THE NEW FACE OF SMALL-TOWN AMERICA

Edgar Sandoval

THE NEW FACE OF
SMALL-TOWN AMERICA

Snapshots of Latino Life in Allentown, Pennsylvania

The Pennsylvania State University Press
University Park, Pennsylvania

Library of Congress
Cataloging-in-Publication Data
Sandoval, Edgar, 1974–
The new face of small-town America : snapshots of Latino life in Allentown, Pennsylvania /
Edgar Sandoval.
p.   cm.
Summary: "A collection of essays on the experiences of Latino immigrants in Allentown,
Pennsylvania"—Provided by publisher.
Includes bibliographical references.
ISBN 978-0-271-03674-8 (cloth : alk. paper)
1. Hispanic Americans—Pennsylvania—Allentown—Social life and customs.
2. Hispanic Americans—Pennsylvania—Allentown—Social conditions.
3. Immigrants—Pennsylvania—Allentown—Social life and customs.
4. Immigrants—Pennsylvania—Allentown—Social conditions.
5. Hispanic Americans—Pennsylvania—Allentown—Biography.
6. Immigrants—Pennsylvania—Allentown—Biography.
7. City and town life—Pennsylvania—Allentown.
8. Allentown (Pa.)—Social life and customs.
9. Allentown (Pa.)—Social conditions.
10. Allentown (Pa.)—Ethnic relations.
I. Title.

F159.A44S25 2010
305.8968′073074827—dc22
2010023591

It is the policy of
The Pennsylvania State University Press
to use acid-free paper.
Publications on uncoated stock satisfy the
minimum requirements of American
National Standard for Information
Sciences—Permanence of Paper for
Printed Library Material,
ANSI Z39.48–1992.

This book is printed on Natures Natural,
which contains 50% post-consumer waste.

CONTENTS

Allentown. Billy Joel. Allentown. Billy Joel. Whenever I told people I was moving to Allentown in the year 2000, people tended to lean back, smile, and recite a few lines from Billy Joel's hit '80s song of the same name, "Allentown." It was almost as if strangers and friends alike rehearsed their reaction to my moving news:

> Every child has a pretty good shot
> To get at least as far as their old man got
> But something happened on the way to that place
> They threw an American flag in our face
> Well I'm living here in Allentown.

I had never heard of such a song, having been raised in Mexico. So I decided to research it, after the insistence of people I knew. "Oh, you have to listen to the song," they told me.

The song describes a town dying slowly, as its factories closed down in the 1980s. Allentown and the greater Lehigh Valley in northeastern Pennsylvania had become stagnant, the song lyrics cried out. It was my turn to find out firsthand.

I made my way to Allentown on a crisp morning in September 2000. At first I thought I had driven to the wrong Allentown, since it was my first time to the Northeast. I had heard of another Allentown in New Jersey, after all. But my confusion was really caused by my song research.

I did not see the closed-down factories and depressed, middle-aged men and women standing out on their porches that Billy Joel sang of, holding their high school diplomas and wondering what they were good for. I saw something completely different. I was told there were Latinos here, sure. That's why I was chosen to come here, to write about them. But I was not ready for what I saw.

I heard salsa blasting from home windows. I saw Puerto Rican flags hanging from doors, cars, and even backpacks. The all-American 7-Elevens had been replaced by bodegas, it seemed. Allentown looked more like a small version of *West Side Story* than an American coal-mining town. Latin-Town seemed a more fitting name.

Yet this was the right Allentown. A few days later, my new newspaper editor, Mary Ellen Alu, walked with me outside the office and pointed to the streets. "We need you to reach out to the Latino community," she told me.

As it turned out, the local Latino residents were not thrilled with their portrayal in the local media. They always appeared to be present when something went awry. And they had the headlines to prove it: stabbings, rowdy parades, poverty, and so on. They were a stereotype, not people with hopes and dreams, they told me.

Many of the white residents weren't crazy about their new neighbors. Latinos had left New York, New Jersey, and Latin America to look for an American way of life in the '80s and '90s. They settled here, but the influx was not without setbacks. Schools weren't ready for Spanish-speaking students, and grades dropped like the winter temperature here. Puerto Rican parades ended in chaos, often with police involvement. Resident-imposed neighborhood segregation quickly followed.

I arrived in the midst of the tension. And so, I grabbed a notebook and took a few deep breaths before I headed out to the streets to start giving a more complete vision of the city's outcasts. I wasn't the only one asking questions, however. The majority of Latinos here come from Caribbean countries. Many of them seemed puzzled by my arrival. They asked, "Where are you from?" "What kind of Spanish accent is that?" "How come they didn't hire a Puerto Rican to cover us?"

In the eyes of the white world here, I was one of them. In the eyes of the community I was hired to write about, I was not really like them. Sure, I spoke their language, shared a similar skin color, and had an accent, not like theirs, but definitely different than the mainstream here. As far as they knew, I was just a foreigner with a similar vocabulary.

I had to brush up on my cultural skills in a hurry. I began to understand that the nice man behind the bakery counter was not calling me bad names—he was asking me if I wanted to buy one of his pastries. (You would be surprised how many words may sound innocent in one Latin culture, but have an offensive meaning in another.) It took some mutual adjustment, but being of Mexican descent proved beneficial. Because I am not Caribbean, cultural differences fascinated and enthralled me. I wrote about Caribbean Latinos the same way an anthropologist writes about a newly discovered culture.

In the end, I'd like to think it all turned out for the best. Latinos began reading about people like them in the newspaper. Members of the mainstream began to learn more about their neighbors, often at the same time I did. Latinos here are doing better than ever before—and local residents recognize their buying power. Latino children are seen as the future now, not the unwanted problem. Allentown now has elected its first Latino immigrant councilman and has seen more Latino professionals and role models than the city has seen in years.

And so here are the stories of the new faces of Allentown. Latinos make up more than a quarter of the city's population, and their numbers continue to grow in the greater Lehigh Valley. But this is not the story of Allentown alone. With the U.S. Census figures showing the arrival of Latinos in more small American cities than ever before, Allentown will continue to serve as an example. Small American cities everywhere have already experienced, or are about to experience, the transformation Allentown saw mostly in this last decade. Few people like change and the unknown. It is only when you become familiar with a foreign concept (or foreigners) that fear disappears and understanding begins. You will discover that behind the accents, ethnic customs, and other cultural differences, we all, as members of the human race, share universal problems and dreams. The Latinos I profiled here want what everybody else wants: to fit in, to prosper, to offer their children a better future, to be recognized as important members of society by the mainstream. They want to coexist. These stories are not just about Latinos in Allentown, after all. They are about Latinos everywhere.

Maybe Billy Joel was right. Allentown had been dormant. Allentown did see a revival. Not the revival everyone hoped for, but one many are learning to accept.

ACKNOWLEDGMENTS

I would like to thank all of the people who helped me, in one way or another, finish this book. All of the people mentioned here provided me with basic necessities—such as inspiration, food, shelter, and alcohol—when I needed it the most. (You know who you are.) Thank you, in no particular order, to Sandra Hernandez, Elvin Cordova, Pedro Hamilton, Lori Sykes, Maira Kraljevic, Colin McKinnon, Gary Kon, Erasmo Guerra, Josh Smith, Jorge Quintana, Shawn Mazata, Frank Lascari, Karen Diaz, and the good people of Allentown; the editorial team at my old newsroom, the *Morning Call*, especially managing editor Dave Erdman and my former line-editor Mary Ellen Alu for helping me craft these stories in the first place; my old photo editor, Ben Morrison, and his team of photographers for helping me illustrate these tales; my unofficial writing coach, Mary Ann Hogan; and of course, my agent, Susan Schulman, for believing that these stories deserved to be reincarnated; my book editor, Sanford G. Thatcher, for being so patient during this process; members of the Latin Alliance, now called Latino Leadership Alliance of the Lehigh Valley; and my family for always being supportive—my parents, Arcelia and Filiberto Sandoval, my brother, Hector, and my sisters, Erica, Mirna, and Mireya.

THE RITUAL

She knows the day will come. She pictures how she will look in her pale yellow gown with spaghetti straps, her Cinderella-like shoes with inch-high heels, her hair pulled into an upsweep and adorned with a tiara.

Part of Nerivonne Sanchez fears the changes her *quinceañera* will bring.

But more so, on the eve of the elaborate fifteenth birthday celebration, she is intrigued about what becoming a young woman will mean. She has attended many of her friends' quinceañeras and has noticed how, almost overnight, they seem different, even changed.

Her fifteen-year-old friends now have weighty matters to consider: perhaps a career and college, a bank account, and other responsibilities. But there is also a giddier side: boys to date, makeup to wear, grown-up parties to attend. She wonders if she will change as fast as they did.

At her quinceañera, she has been told, she will be presented as a young woman to family and friends. From that time on, she will be expected to leave behind her childlike qualities.

But stop being a child? That thought makes Nerivonne a little uneasy. Being a child is what she knows. She looks cherubic—her face round like a full moon and her skin as smooth as a baby's. Her bedroom is decorated with Tweety Bird stuffed toys, towels, posters, and stickers.

Dresses? She can't chase her little brother if she's wearing one. She prefers jeans, T-shirts, and tennis shoes. Long nails? They will get in her way when she wants to dial the phone or play video games. Makeup? She is not looking for a boyfriend. Well, unless action star Vin Diesel or a member of the boy band B2K asks.

"I'm not sure if I am ready to become a woman," she says before the big night. "I want to be a child longer."

Her parents have tried to explain to her what being a quinceañera will mean. As far as the Sanchezes know, Latino families have always celebrated a daughter's fifteenth birthday celebration as an important milestone. It's a passage from childhood to adulthood. In the old days it used to mean a girl had become a woman and was ready for marriage and children.

The Sanchezes don't want her to marry, of course, they explained. But it will be time for her to take on more womanly tasks, such as doing the dishes and helping around the house more. No more cartoons and child's play. That's how Nerivonne's mother and grandmother knew that they had become women. Now it is her turn.

Like most, Nerivonne's celebration will have a religious component. A religious leader, often a Catholic priest, will bless the fifteen-year-old, typically dressed in a princesslike gown. Then, in a ceremony that resembles a seventh-century court dance, she is presented to society as a young woman. Nerivonne does like that part, because it reminds her of Cinderella.

The Transformation

Nerivonne is nervous when she wakes up around 9 a.m. on November 16, a cold and rainy Saturday and the day of her quinceañera. She turned fifteen three days earlier, but that day went on without much fanfare. She feels that today is her real birthday.

An invitation has Tweety on the outside, holding flowers and saying, "I tawt of you today! I did! I did!" Inside, in blue ink, she wrote "Mis 15 Años." She had chosen the cards from the children's section of a party store, instead of those that pictured a young woman in a fancy gown.

Nerivonne puts on black jeans and a red Tweety Bird T-shirt. She is comfortable. Silently she thanks her parents and her paternal grandparents for this special day.

Her parents, who work at Apple's Market in Allentown, could not afford an upscale bash. But with help from Nerivonne's paternal grandparents they saved about $1,000 for the event, buying a gown, shoes, and elbow-length gloves, along with decorations at a dollar store, paying for a disc jockey, and renting a large room at the Hispanic American Organization on Fourth Street in downtown Allentown.

Her grandmother and other relatives will prepare the feast: Puerto Rican–style rice, beans and pork, chicken, and rolled and fried tacos, enough food to feed about one hundred family members and friends.

She will wear a tiara and jewelry borrowed from a cousin in Florida, who celebrated her quinceañera years ago.

"It may not be the fanciest party," Nerivonne remembers her grandmother, Evelyn Marrero, saying. "But it is with all of our love, and that is what counts. Love. Not money."

By 2 p.m. Nerivonne's transformation begins. Her first stop is a nail salon on Seventh Street, a few blocks from her home in center city. Nerivonne gets fake nails and a French manicure.

"This is the first time I get professional nails," she tells her cousin Frances Rivera on the way back to her house, admiring her nails. "I got them for free because I told him it was my quinceañera."

They giggle.

Frances, who is visiting from Connecticut, understands Nerivonne's excitement. She will celebrate her quinceañera in two weeks.

Back at home, it's time for a new hairdo.

"I have just the look for you," Frances tells her, and the girls head upstairs.

The house is bustling. Nerivonne's younger brother, Felix, is playing a wrestling video game, screaming as his player takes a beating from an opponent that his cousin maneuvers via remote.

Nerivonne's mother, Ivonne Rodriguez, hurries through the upstairs yelling, "We still need to pick up your balloons, Nerivonne! Who is taking care of that?"

Family friend Jazmin Crespo, who will apply the makeup, runs behind her one-year-old daughter, who is picking up pennies from the floor and putting them in her mouth.

Nerivonne's father, Valeriano Sanchez, rushes to the bathroom to take a shower. Salsa music blasts from the downstairs living room.

The chaos does not seem to bother Nerivonne. She sits still as her cousin styles her hair, combing it back, ponytail-style, and sweeping part of her hair left across her forehead. A little bit of hair gel keeps it intact.

"Just like a princess," Frances says.

Nerivonne moves to her mother's bedroom, where Crespo waits with a case of makeup. Crespo applies soft pink eye shadow, peach foundation, and chocolate brown lipstick. Nerivonne holds back giggles as the makeup brush glides over her cheeks. It tickles.

"We want you to look sexy, but not too sexy, because she is only fifteen," Crespo says to nobody in particular.

The buzz over the new hairstyle and the makeup lures relatives to the bedroom.

"Where is my daughter? They changed my daughter," her mother jokes. "Oh, I don't want to cry now."

"Wow. You are all grown up now," says her uncle, Nelson Bermudez, who traveled from Puerto Rico for the quinceañera.

"You look like Queen Elizabeth," says her brother.

"This is the first time I see you with makeup," Crespo interrupts. "Girl, you bangin'."

Nerivonne walks to the living room, her nails, hair, and makeup done.

She has a few hours to kill before heading to the celebration. She turns on the TV to keep her mind off the party. She flips channels. "Looney Tunes," she says.

A few seconds later she realizes that adults are in the room. Maybe cartoons are not such a good idea anymore. She flips the channel and finds *The Wedding Planner* with Jennifer Lopez. A better option, she thinks.

"Jeez, I got the ending." She flips to more channels.

"I can't do anything with these nails," she says and turns off the TV.

The Night Is Here

"It's time to go. Time to go!" Nerivonne's mother screams at about 7:30 p.m. as she walks from the kitchen to the living room.

This is it, Nerivonne tells herself. Her heart beats faster. Her stomach tightens. More people arrive, mostly girls her age wearing stylish gowns.

Since it's raining, Nerivonne decides to change into her new gown—yellow like Tweety Bird, but not as bright—at the Hispanic American Organization building. She doesn't want to get it wet.

Her grandmother eagerly waits for her there. "I want you all to leave," she tells a group of curious teens and children. "You cannot see her with her dress until she walks into the dance room. Go!"

Nerivonne walks into the bathroom with her grandmother, who unwraps the gown. Nerivonne stares at it. She remembers when she bought it earlier at a bridal store in Whitehall Township. It had taken her just a few minutes to find the one she liked.

"That one, 'buela. That one!" Nerivonne said to her grandmother as soon as she spotted it on a rack.

When she tried it on, her mother wept. Her grandmother prayed. All were excited.

Now the big night has arrived. Nerivonne has never been particularly fond of dresses, but she longs to wear this gown. Maybe, she thinks, it's a sign she is already growing into a woman.

"You look so beautiful," her grandmother tells her when she dons her gown.

Nerivonne looks at herself in the bathroom mirror. People had called her cute, chubby, chatty. But tonight family and friends will describe her as beautiful, gorgeous, sexy.

She likes the new look.

"I feel different. I just do," she says.

She hides from her friends and relatives in a hall adjacent to the building's cafeteria, which has been turned into a ballroom for the special night.

Bermudez, her uncle, will escort her.

Her grandmother will let her know when it is time to enter the room. Not just yet.

Nerivonne's friends and their dates enter first, one by one. Her parents follow. Then, her grandmother, holding a microphone, announces, "This night we gather to celebrate Nerivonne's fifteen years. Another step in her life."

Nerivonne, smiling, walks in with her uncle, linking her arm in his. She feels a mix of emotions. Nervousness. Excitement. Happiness. Some sadness. But the moment is magical.

Her father makes eye contact and returns a smile. Her mother cries. Her grandmother nods "yes," as if answering the question Nerivonne has in her mind: "Is this really happening?" Her best friends clap as she walks past them.

Tweety balloons hang from the ceiling and yellow tablecloths cover the tables. The disc jockey plays "Tiempo de Vals," a waltz from Puerto Rican pop star Chayanne and a standard at quinceañeras. Sure, Nerivonne has danced to salsa and hip-hop in her living room. But this is different. She is slow dancing with her uncle in front of her parents and guests—a grown-up dance.

One custom calls for the fifteen-year-old's father to carry a pair of high-heeled shoes on a cushion so his daughter can change from her flats for the father-daughter dance. But Nerivonne did not want to do this. It seemed fancy. She is not a fancy girl.

Her father steps in, taking over for Nerivonne's uncle.

Her mother stands nearby holding a stuffed Tweety with a Santa hat and stocking. Those who want to be part of the first dance with Nerivonne slip a dollar or two into the stocking. Her grandfather steps in, then a boy from school, her cousins and her girlfriends.

A few minutes later, the disc jockey plays salsa and people begin dancing on their own. Nerivonne feels less pressure. Fewer eyes on her. The buffet is set up in an adjoining kitchen.

Nerivonne takes off her shoes and dances the *culebra*, or snake dance, leading guests in a chain dance around the room.

When it's time to cut the cake, Nerivonne hurries over to her mother and warns her, "Don't cut Tweety Bird from the cake. I don't want people to eat him!"

After receiving a blessing from Father Andy Gehringer of Sacred Heart Church, from Fourth Street, Nerivonne addresses her guests. Her hand is shaking as she grabs the microphone. She thanks her parents for being there for her and for having the quinceañera, every Latina's dream, even though they struggled to put the money together. All three hug and shed tears of happiness.

"And what, you forgot about your grandparents?" asks her grandmother, putting her hands on her hips.

"No, I love you too," Nerivonne says, hugging her grandparents. They toast with sangria, raising plastic cups. Nerivonne takes a sip and makes a funny face. It's sour. So this is what alcohol tastes like, she tells herself.

She opens presents and envelopes with $10 and $20 bills, about $80 in all, the most money she has seen at one time.

After about three hours, some guests begin to leave.

Her shoes off, Nerivonne and three friends hold hands and walk to the dance floor one last time. They sing a nursery rhyme:

> Ring around the rosy,
> A pocket full of posies,
> Ashes! Ashes!
> We all fall down.

The girls collapse to the floor, giggling. It will take more than one night for Nerivonne to adjust to womanhood.

Intruder

In journalism school, I was taught not to get too close to sources. Try telling that to the Sanchez family.

I met the Sanchezes in late 2002 while researching a piece about quinceañeras. Nerivonne Sanchez was about to turn fifteen.

I went to the family's house knowing what to expect, to some extent. Living among and writing about Latinos for a living, I knew that most Latinos tend to be warm and welcoming.

But I made my rules clear. I would follow them and ask annoying questions. I could not accept food or presents. That would be unethical. I couldn't get too close with them either. That would blur our roles. We shook hands and sealed our deal.

Nerivonne's grandmother came out of the kitchen and offered me baked bread stuffed with meat. "You want to eat empanadas? They are good. I just made them," Evelyn Marrero asked.

"Oh, no, thank you," I said. "I can't, because of my job."

"Why, you can't eat? What kind of job is that?" she said, shaking her head. The rules I had just explained weren't sinking in.

Over the next few weeks, the family and I got to know each other better. I stopped by the Sanchezes' house every now and then and tried to be there when they were making plans for the celebration. By the time of the quinceañera, I went from being called "Edgar with the *Morning Call* [the Allentown newspaper]" to simply "Edgar." I was too close. There was no way back.

I have faced similar situations many times before while covering the area's Latino community. I insist on playing a reporter role. Some of my sources insist I am a Latino first. It is a never-ending battle.

I walked in and out of the Sanchez home, helped myself to a cup of coffee and used the bathroom without asking. Sure, give me an empanada and one for the way home, I would tell the grandmother.

How could I not? It would have been an insult not to take the food being offered. They might think I considered myself too good for their food. Besides, my editors knew I don't cook, never have, and probably never will. I will die of starvation before I pick up a pan.

On the day of the quinceañera, Nerivonne's mother, Ivonne Rodriguez, needed help picking up empanadas. "Edgar, you look strong enough. Follow me," she said.

I wanted to say, hey, hold on. I'm here just to observe. Instead, we walked to a neighbor's house, and she loaded me with a large tray of empanadas. "This way," she told me.

Once at the ballroom, I wanted to sit down and observe and take notes. The Sanchez family had other plans. Nerivonne danced her first waltz with her uncle, father, and friends. Nerivonne's mom kept glancing at me and signaling me to dance with her daughter. I pretended my eyes were itching and did not see her.

Then the disc jockey played some salsa. She walked over to my table. "You are dancing with my daughter," she said firmly.

That was that. I got up. A group of teen girls stood in a corner and giggled. I stood in front of Nerivonne. How close is too close? But Nerivonne was not worried. She began dancing to the music.

"I'm not a good dancer," I told her.

She nodded.

Well, let's not rush to agree, I thought.

Some girls were standing beside us. "Are you killing roaches with your feet?" one of them asked me in Spanish.

The song, which seemed to last hours, was finally over. I walked to my table. My heart began beating more slowly; the public humiliation was over. I was going to sit back and enjoy the rest of the ceremony. Right before I sat down I heard Nerivonne's grandmother calling my name over the microphone. Wait, *my* name?

"We want Edgar to stand beside the cake with Nerivonne. Today is his birthday, and he decided to spend it with us," she said to the crowd and they all looked at me, knowing who I was. I was, after all, the only weirdo zooming around Nerivonne, writing down every one of her moves, as if the safety of the planet depended on it.

I turned tomato red and felt my face burning. I stood beside Nerivonne. The newspaper's photographer took some shots of Nerivonne standing in front of the cake. He looked at me and shook his head, as if saying, "Move, so I can take her photo."

I tried to walk very slowly away from Nerivonne but her mother blocked my way.

"Don't be so shy," she said. "Stay there. I want you to share this moment with us."

In the end, I learned that journalism rules don't always apply when you write about everyday folks. So I ate their empanadas, and I danced with the main subject of my piece, and I ate a dish that her grandmother prepared for me, Mexican taquitos.

That got me a little close to them. But in the end, that only made my piece better. I was able to better understand Nerivonne and her feelings as she went through her rite of passage. Besides, I was not the only one receiving warm affection from the Sanchezes. At their house a few days after the party, Nerivonne was showing her quinceañera photos to a man who had walked in to sell them a life insurance policy.

Nobody can escape the Sanchezes' charm.

2

A PRINCIPAL DUTY

Principal David Vazquez takes a deep breath, and for a few moments, enjoys the quiet of an early morning inside the Roberto Clemente Charter School.

It's 7 a.m., still dark outside, and Vazquez is the first to arrive at the Allentown charter school that targets at-risk students, mostly Latino. It's located in the Hispanic American Organization building downtown.

Vazquez, still in his first days as principal, knows that as the day unfolds, he'll probably have to deal with disciplinary issues, such as boys and girls fighting with each other in the cafeteria or arguing with teachers, and administrative issues, such as searching for grants to develop more educational and mentoring programs.

At the end of each day, Vazquez says, "I always tell myself, 'This day was better than yesterday.'"

This was a job he had not expected to take, back in 2001 when the school was just a few months old. He still wanted to finish his master's degree in education, spend time with his family, and, well, so many other things. But he could not resist the message he received from the school founders that cold winter night in 2001. The school's first principal, Claudio Cerullo, had resigned after just two and a half weeks to care for his ailing mother.

There was more. Some of the girls' uniforms arrived weeks late because officials missed an ordering deadline. The school bought a bus, but couldn't run it for two months as it struggled to find a qualified driver. The lockers arrived about three weeks late, requiring the nearly one hundred students to carry their books and materials all day long. As the school searched for a licensed bus driver, many students had to walk several blocks to and from school almost every day.

How could he say no to these children who needed him? He remembered that the school had been named after the late Pittsburgh Pirates baseball star. The name serves as a symbol of pride and hope among inner-city children, he knows. After all, the children would ask themselves, if Clemente, a son of poor Puerto Rican farmers, could make it so high up, why couldn't they? Clemente was the first great Latin American player to captivate the major leagues. But also, still thinking of Clemente's influence on Latinos, if the children from poor and broken homes had high aspirations, why couldn't he help the school stay afloat and do better?

And so he took the job. He had been an administrator for a community college. How different could it be?

The school is not all alone. When it opened, it used to get about $677,000 from the Allentown School District. Most of that money goes to staff salary. Teachers earn between $30,000 and $40,000. School founders borrowed $21,000 to help pay for the bus and lockers. The school also got a jump-start of $30,000 from a Lehigh Valley philanthropist, Linny Fowler, for a new bus stamped with the number Clemente wore in right field—21. Administrators are always looking for grants to support new programs and materials.

"The school is running smoother now," Vazquez admits.

Clemente is the only charter school operating in Lehigh and Northampton counties. There are more than 1,700 charter schools nationwide, including close to 70 in Pennsylvania.

On this Thursday morning, Vazquez unlocks the school's glass front doors and waits for bus 21 to arrive. Sometimes Vazquez rides the bus with the students to make sure they behave. But as time goes by, the driver has reported more improved behavior among the youths, many who live nearby in center-city Allentown, the most urban area in the Lehigh Valley.

"They need so much help, these kids," he says, walking to his office first thing in the morning. "We need to focus not only on improving their academic achievements but also on the emotional baggage they carry."

Students' dropping out is not new here. Some move to other cities, or other neighborhoods, and others dislike the school's uniform policy and go back to public school.

Vazquez says he's not surprised by the behavior problems that surfaced during his first days. He even expected them. The children wanted to test him. They were loud in the classroom, and fought in the halls and the cafeteria. Many forgot or refused to wear the school uniform: khaki pants or plaid skirts, white shirt, blue tie, and blue blazer.

Juanita Galarza, one of the school mothers, tells him she likes that her sons wear uniforms. She remembers when she used to attend school in her native Puerto Rico and schoolmates used to tease her for not wearing the latest name brands.

"There is no issue like that here," Galarza tells him. "All the students look the same. I don't want them to feel less, like I did. I want them to come to school and focus on learning."

Slowly, Vazquez says, the school is making progress, despite those critics who say Latinos are separating themselves from the rest of the Allentown student body by creating a charter school. Latinos make up more than half of the Allentown School District student population. Here, at the charter school, almost 100 percent are Latinos. Just a handful are white and African American.

"It just so happens that the disadvantaged students tend to be from Latino families," he says. "Everyone is welcomed to this school."

It's 9 a.m., the first class period is not yet over, and already two students are sitting outside Vazquez's office. One did not wear her uniform, and the other walked out of her classroom without permission. Now, for not following rules, they have to spend the rest of the school day in the lobby, he sternly tells them.

"I want to be able to teach children how to follow rules," Vazquez says. "Some parents even say I am too lenient."

As days go by, fewer students are being disciplined for bad behavior, but Vazquez has learned to accept that children will be children, always energetic.

"They seem to have more school pride now," he says. "Some of these students have tough situations at home. We have to help them emotionally and academically."

English teacher Angela Georgis, who is in her late twenties, admits that she showed up for her first day at work expecting a group of rowdy children. But throughout her first morning here her students seem to have been listening and taking notes.

"Maybe they are just testing me," says Georgis. She filled the position of an English teacher who quit at the end of the first semester to take another job. "I expected to end the morning with a sore throat."

The first goal of the school staff is to get the behavior problems under control. Once that is done, Vazquez and his staff will focus more and more on raising the students' academic levels. After all, there is always the growing need to do well on the Pennsylvania System of School Assessment test, which is used to evaluate school districts in Pennsylvania.

"We know we are probably not going to do that well. We are so new," Vazquez says. "We need time to begin proving ourselves."

Vazquez spent his first few months bringing in programs and new software to help children learn writing, reading, math, and other subjects and encouraging outside mentors to spend time working with the children.

Jesus Rodriguez is a special education teacher in his fifties. Like him, most of his co-workers try to find creative ways to get the children's attention. To get his students interested in math and geometry, he asked them to build a small bridge and other projects. Students use mathematical and geometry equations to build their projects.

"It's not gonna work if I just stand there and start talking about math," Rodriguez says.

Those are the kinds of creative teaching methods Vazquez encourages. Those who work with Vazquez have noticed his determination to get children interested in school and the countless hours he spends visiting parents and children after school.

"He is always looking for ways to bring more educational programs to the school," says Lupe Pearce, the school's chief administrative officer. "We are starting to see good results in the children."

"We are always looking for ways to bring more money to the school," she goes on. "Community expectations are very high for the only charter school in the

Lehigh Valley, and we feel like we do really have to work. But being the new school, starting from scratch, we have come a long way."

The Clemente school also turns in an annual review to the Allentown School Board. However, the district does not monitor the charter school, which is mandated by the state to operate independently.

Higher Ed

Ever since Vazquez took the job, he had a single goal in mind: to encourage youths to go to college. After all, he did. He earned his bachelor's degree in business and education from the Inter-American University of Puerto Rico in San Juan in 1990. He also has a master's in bilingual education from Adelphi University. He had worked as an administrative intern at nearby educational institutions, like Clearview Elementary School in Bethlehem, and ran a literacy program for Northampton Community College, the county next door.

I'm here to stay for a long time, he tells himself. And I will be their role model.

Shortly before noon, Vazquez tries to make a quick stop at the school cafeteria to check on the children. The moment he steps in, he hears an announcement over the loudspeaker, asking for him at the front desk. He walks out, and two boys begin punching each other in the cafeteria.

Science teacher Joseph Grello runs to separate them.

Vazquez hears about the fight a few minutes later when Grello takes the students to his office. Vazquez, who directs the students to spend the rest of the day in the school's lobby, glances at his watch.

"This is nothing," he says. "Today is a quiet day."

Some students say it took a while to get used to a new school. But as time went on, they got to know almost all the students and teachers on a first-name basis. Most classrooms average twelve students.

"I like smaller classrooms," says Jessica Grachi, an eighth-grader. "You get to ask more questions and make friends faster."

Courses are taught in English, although Spanish can be heard among students and staff in the halls and cafeteria.

About 3 p.m., at the end of the school day, after meeting with parents, children, and staff members, Vazquez tries to get something to eat. His secretary leaves him a cold plate of Puerto Rican rice and ham in the refrigerator of the second-floor cafeteria.

"My favorite," he says.

He meets yet another parent and closes the door. The bell rings, and the children leave their classrooms.

"It has been a good day," he says. "Tomorrow, I'm sure, I will do it all over again."

3

SPANISH SOUND BITES

Every weeknight Edith Morales has a date at 11 p.m. Once you turn seventy, she'd tell you, you need to go to bed early and get up early. She changed her routine in early 2003, ignoring her own advice, when the local television news station WFMZ began airing the first-ever Spanish-language broadcast in northeast Pennsylvania and southwest New Jersey.

Now she makes sure she sets her alarm for just before 11 p.m. When the alarm wakes her up, she splashes some water on her face to stay awake and then makes her way to the living room downstairs. The walk can be slow, since she has a bad knee.

She settles her petite frame into a puffy white couch. She switches to WFMZ, channel 69. The English-language news anchors are usually still chitchatting to kill the last few seconds. And then, moments later, as if the television set switched channels by itself, the mood and tone on air changes.

A young Latino man appears—Jorge Quintana, the Spanish-language edition's main news anchor.

"Tan lindo," she says, calling him good looking.

"Esta noche en su edicion en Espanol . . ." (Tonight on your edition of the Spanish language news . . .), Quintana announces, and Morales focuses all her attention on what he has to say.

It's no surprise that Morales and many other area Latinos are eager for a news source in their language. Ever since Latinos began populating the area in bigger numbers, beginning in the '80s and '90s in Philadelphia, southwest New Jersey, the Lehigh Valley, and Berks County, they have lacked a daily Spanish-language news outlet. There are several weekly publications in Spanish. They, however, offer local advertising and commentary, not daily news information.

"For those who understand English, that's fine, they have news channels in their language," says Morales, who has lived in Allentown for thirty-five years. "But for those of us who don't, all we have is thirty minutes at 11 p.m."

WFMZ could not ignore the burgeoning number of Latinos in the area, said Brad Reinhart, the station's news director. Latinos make up more than a quarter of the population in Allentown and are already the majority in the neighboring city of Reading.

"While we are firm believers in the value of having Americans share a common language, news demands immediacy," Reinhart said. "The fundamental of local news cannot wait while immigrants learn English."

The news station as a whole reaches more than 350,000 viewers on an average day, on both cable and local television, in both English and Spanish.

The Spanish-language newscast comprises its anchor, Quintana; two reporters, Perla Lopez Baray and Fior D. Hernandez; a weather reporter, Zendy Caicedo Tintle; and a news producer, Javier Palmera. All of them are veterans of the news business, having reported the news in the Southwest and in Florida. But they are also young, in their late twenties and early thirties.

Their viewers, they all agree, are more than just viewers. They are also people, like Morales, who look to them as role models. Their viewers refer to each of the broadcasters by their first names. Television has that power, Quintana and his cast know—and studies show that Latinos tend to prefer broadcast news to print news outlets.

The newscasters have become the closest thing to Latino celebrities the area has seen. They are often asked to speak at social engagements and appear in the social pages of the Spanish-language weeklies.

"It's strange. People always remember what I wear on a certain day," Tintle says, amused. "They feel free to tell me when what I wear looks good. Or when I look like a fifty-year-old woman."

Baray says that people often tell her she looks much more petite in person. "Most of all, the girls always ask me if Jorge [Quintana] is single," she says. "All of the girls want to go out with him. I don't tell them. That's private."

Behind the local glamour, there are serious news stories to cover. On an average day, the cast meets at 6 p.m. to discuss the news of the day. Because they are a small staff, reporters must deliver a story every day. Hernandez oversees the Berks County area, Baray keeps an eye on the Philadelphia region, and Quintana anchors and often reports out of the Lehigh Valley, or where needed. Sometimes they use some of the big stories aired earlier in their English-language edition. But the Spanish-language crew focuses on stories that cater to Latinos, such as news about immigration laws.

On this night, after the English-language newscast has aired its 10 p.m. and 10:30 p.m. editions, the English-speaking cast members acknowledge Quintana, as he waits patiently for their show to end. Once they are done, Quintana settles in his chair, taking one last look at his hair and adjusting his suit. He looks at the camera and begins another busy newscast.

"More than thirty undocumented immigrants in Northampton County face deportation," he says. His speaks slowly and tries to withhold all emotion while on air. That's the number-one rule of broadcast news, he knows. Facts only, not emotions.

"They appeared today in court," he goes on. "The majority pleaded guilty of using fake documents to work."

Off the air, he will tell you that these are the stories that touch him the most and that convinced him to get into "the business" to begin with. As a child, Quintana dreamed of becoming a Spanish-literature professor. Yet he had always been curious about the world of *la tele* (short for *la television*, the television). He got a job as a news producer in New Mexico and quickly rose to become a news reporter. Because he was one of the few Spanish speakers at the station, he was often asked to cover stories along the Mexico–United States border. That's when he realized he wanted to give a voice to those who did not have it, people like his mother, a Spanish-speaking native of Nicaragua. Quintana himself is an immigrant, arriving in the United States at age eleven. He first lived in California, and then educated himself in the Las Vegas area.

"I made the switch to the Spanish market," he says, still off-air. "I wanted to tell stories of people who have gone through what I have gone through."

That's a feeling shared by his fellow newscasters. Baray says that she often feels frustration while on the job. Many of her news sources in peril come to her for help, especially those who share her Mexican nationality. They feel an unspoken bond, she says.

"Often, I can't do much. They see me on TV and think I have all this power," she says, with a tone of disappointment. "I'm not a lawyer or a judge. I'm not a law expert. All I can do is tell their stories and get all sides." Learning to walk the fine line between being a local Latino icon and a newsperson is something they struggle to cope with day after day, the newscasters all agree.

When Quintana passes on the story about the immigrants to Baray, she appears on screen on a prerecorded tape and tells viewers: "Handcuffed and lowering their heads, sixteen undocumented immigrants appeared before a judge."

Seconds later she then offers her microphone to one of the accused, Teodoro Perez.

"Truth is, I feel guilty," he tells her, his eyes cast down in shame.

"Did you know you were committing a crime?" she asks.

"Yes."

"Did you do it out of need?"

"Yes, the need."

But not all is gloomy news. Latinos are known for their passion for life, upbeat tempos, and good food. And that's part of what the news team wants to transmit, they say.

For this broadcast, Hernandez had been covering the grand opening of one of the first galleries showcasing all the art done by Latinos at the Regional Center for the Arts in Reading. Quintana goes live to her.

"Jorge. There is a tremendous explosion of Latino art," Hernandez says, never losing her smile. "Puerto Rico, Colombia, El Salvador, and the Dominican Republic are among the countries represented here."

In her story, the colorful art is accompanied by the popular song "Oye como va" as the Latin artists talk about their art. Some of them showcase paintings of tropical settings. Another shows a farm worker growing coffee and fruit.

"Right now I'm using a lot of color. The color of our lands," one of the artists tells Hernandez. "Art is universal. It has no language. Everyone is welcome."

The newscast ends a few minutes later and the cast meets to review the ups and downs of the day's edition. Everyone likes Hernandez's upbeat story. They all agree they need more of that—stories with colorful images, catchy music in the background, and stories of Latinos in a positive light. The first piece was well done, they agree. Then they go home to get their sleep before they do it all over again the next day.

In her living room, at now 11:30 p.m., Edith Morales thinks that the end of the newscast is bittersweet. The story of the farm workers made her feel sad, seeing all those men in shackles.

"I feel bad for them. They are just trying to feed their families, not cause trouble," she says.

Overall, however, Morales wishes the newscast lasted more than half an hour. She heads to bed, counting the hours until she will get to see people like her in her nightly news again, no matter how late they appear.

Jorge Quintana has since left the station to pursue public relations outside Atlanta, Georgia, where he leads a school district's newscast.

4

HOME AWAY FROM HOME

Alfredo Sanchez glances at his watch as he pulls his employer's miniature school bus up to the curb on South Chestnut Street, a small street in this rusty town. The morning fog gives the street the illusion of a scary movie set. Most homes are small and made out of wood. Some are deteriorating.

It's 6:30 a.m. and Sanchez has come to pick up friends he knows from Los Campos, Mexico, and take them to work in the tree fields near Catawissa, Columbia County.

Four men wearing long-sleeved shirts, jeans, caps, and work boots sleepily walk out of a spartan but well-kept row home. Some are rubbing their eyes.

"¡Ya vamonos!" Sanchez shouts. (Let's go!)

Some of the workers fall back to sleep as Sanchez stops for six more men a few blocks away, then continues on the forty-minute drive uphill and over narrow roads. They will be happy for the extra rest once they get to the fields, where, for eight hours, they will trim pine trees under an unforgiving sun.

Sanchez and his friends had never really planned on coming here to Shenandoah, a gritty, coal-mining borough in Schuylkill County known for its frozen pierogies and as the hometown of big band greats Tommy and Jimmy Dorsey. They did not even know where it was on a map. But, like a few others before them, they were lured here by work opportunities and inexpensive housing. They liked it here because of its central location between the factories and rich valleys of Schuylkill and Columbia counties and the orchards and farms of Lehigh County.

Seemingly overnight, longtime residents—mostly white and of European ancestry—began seeing groups of darker-skinned men and women walking their streets, speaking Spanish, displaying a different culture.

"At first I did not care for them at all," said Rita Karlavage, a native of Shenandoah in her mid-forties. "I was afraid of them. But some of them are nice. They just need to start speaking English. Their lives would be much easier if they did."

"We are beginning to see a trend that you saw mostly in urban areas," borough manager Joseph L. Palubinsky said. "People [longtime residents] have never seen Hispanics before in their lives, before they started coming here."

Promised Land

As a child in Los Campos, Sanchez considered the United States a faraway promised land, a place men traveled to and returned from with a wallet full of green bills that bought cars, clothes, and two-story houses.

He wanted to be like those men. But he also loved his small town in central Mexico, where everyone knew everyone else, where, just a few blocks away, he would eventually meet the woman he would marry.

But by age nineteen, Sanchez decided to leave his home for work in the United States. He first went to the fields of North Carolina. A friend there told him about Shenandoah. Jobs paid about the same, but rent was cheaper. There were more opportunities to save money, the friend told him.

Sanchez had no idea where Shenandoah was, but the offer sounded good. So, eleven years ago, he ventured to eastern Pennsylvania and moved to the town of Numidia, in Columbia County.

He, in turn, told people back home in the Mexican state of Aguascalientes about work in the tree fields, and they followed him. Most of them were like him, young men in their twenties and early thirties: Jose de Jesus Ortiz Gomez, Abelardo Lopez, Juan de la Rosa, Ramiro Arellano, and Alfredo's brother, Daniel Sanchez.

They like the work. Their employer, Abraczinskas Nurseries, Inc., in Catawissa, has work for them most of the year, finds them housing in Shenandoah, and pays the rent.

The owners are a few of the nice "gringos" (as they put it) in the area, Sanchez and his friends agree.

The work season is typically ten months, March through December. The men work eight hours a day, from five to seven days a week. Entry-level jobs pay $6 to $6.50 an hour or more, depending on the worker's seniority. Most of the men make about $240 a week. They manage to save about $300 a month and send it back to their families.

The money buys more in Mexico than in the United States. What they spend to buy groceries for one week here would buy one month's worth of groceries in Mexico.

"You make just enough to live here and send back home," Lopez says. "But I did not go to school, so what can I expect? In Mexico, you make a lot less and work a lot harder."

Lopez bought a blue 1979 Nissan for $1,300 that he left in Mexico to drive when he gets back home. He also has managed to restore the floor of his parents' home in Mexico with the money he made.

But the money comes at a price, they know. Sanchez and his friends don't feel welcome in Shenandoah, a square-mile borough of 5,624 people.

"People here do not like us," Alfredo Sanchez says. "I don't understand. They don't know us."

Sanchez doesn't understand because he knows that they have much in common. Many residents and their parents, and perhaps even their grandparents, were European immigrants who came to Shenandoah looking for work in the coal mines early in the 1900s. Now, when Sanchez and some of his friends want to find work and better their lives, they find hostility.

Sanchez says that he does not want much—just people to smile at him in the streets and greet him like they would anybody else. He does not want to be followed when he enters a store. He does not like it when some people spit on a sidewalk where he just walked. He does not want teenagers calling him names he does not understand but that must be bad because of the tone of their voice.

"We want to be like anybody else," he says.

Librarian Theresa Kolonsky, in her mid-sixties, knows how the Mexican newcomers feel. Her parents arrived from Italy in the early 1900s to the borough settled by Polish, Irish, German, British, and other European immigrants. Shenandoah had about 30,000 residents at the time. Those who spoke English, such as the Irish and British, usually got the better jobs in the mines, Kolonsky remembers. An Italian person would not dare walk into a Polish section of the borough. "Things would get ugly," she said.

Decades later, Kolonsky is seeing a mirror of the hardships her family endured. "It's the same story repeating itself," she said. "A lot of the people who do not like the Mexicans went through the same thing, but it seems like they have already forgotten that."

Sanchez shakes his head as he and his crew arrive at Catawissa, outside the Abraczinskas office. A larger bus with other workers, including migrant workers from Central America, will take them to the nearby field to trim evergreens, many of which will be sold as Christmas trees come December.

"We come here to work, and that is what we are going to do," Sanchez tells his friends. "Yeah," they say collectively. "Work."

Ed Freeman, one of the tree farm operators, does not understand the tension he hears about between the small number of workers living in the area and the larger community.

Welcoming the Latino migrant workers is more than pure economics. He has become a friend of some of the workers, such as Sanchez.

Around 1912, Freeman's grandfather had a vision of planting trees for the Christmas season. But it was not until 1950 that he got serious and began to plant more trees.

Now, six brothers and cousins who run the business own and operate about 2,500 acres, and they ship trees throughout the East Coast. In the past, the company has shipped trees to Puerto Rico, Mexico, Bermuda, and areas west of Chicago. Never in his career has Freeman seen better workers than the migrants from Mexico and other Latin American countries.

"Truth is, the Hispanics produce much more than the Americans," Freeman says. "One Hispanic can do the work of three or four Americans. I have seen that over and over. Americans do not want to work in the heat.

"Americans like to eat their vegetables and fruit, but they never stop to think who picked them up for them," he says. "They eat because of the Hispanics who do the work they do not want to do."

Padre Potts

When Shenandoah residents talk about the Mexican workers, they bring up one name: Father Robert Potts.

"People blame Father Potts," says Palubinsky, the borough manager. "People said he brought them here and a lot of them don't like that." Potts is aware of the criticism. "No, no," he says, he did not bring anybody here.

He sits to eat his dinner at St. George Catholic Church rectory, one of three churches to which he ministers.

"They come here and I help them," he says softly. "I help people and it does not matter what language they speak or what their background is. That is my duty."

Potts and Sister Helen McGroarty have become more than spiritual leaders for the growing Mexican community.

Many of the migrant workers knock on their doors when they need advice. Potts and McGroarty help them prepare cultural events. Potts continues to learn Spanish in order to offer Mass in their language every Sunday.

When about seventeen migrant workers suffered a car accident in July 2001, in which two of them died, Potts and McGroarty felt as if they had lost two of their own.

Potts visited the survivors at the hospital and collected money and goods from people in the Lehigh Valley and Shenandoah to help them while they recovered. McGroarty, who was caring for her ailing father in Allentown, also went to their side.

Potts hears about the migrants' fears. Immigration agents constantly drive through the borough. Some of the workers have brought their families and have settled in the community, enrolling their children in the school district, where they make up a small percentage of the student body.

But the majority are still lone men, who come in groups and share apartments or older homes, looking for work.

At a Sunday Mass, Potts dedicates part of his sermon to those who died in the accident in Lynn Township and those recovering from their injuries. He stands in front of the altar at Our Lady of Mount Carmel Church.

About seventy churchgoers, mostly Mexican families, listen to his sermon in Spanish: "Let's ask God to heal the relatives of those who died and heal the wounds of the injured. Let's ask God for those who work in the fields, so that one day they will have their reward," Potts tells them in broken Spanish, his eyes half-closed. "Let's ask God so that this whole town can get along."

Far Afield

In the fields, Sanchez focuses on why he came to Pennsylvania: to support his wife and his elementary-school-aged daughter.

Sanchez takes a short break and pulls out a picture of his wife, Raquel, a beautiful woman with pitch-black hair and caramel-colored skin, and his daughter, Lucero, whose name means "bright star."

His wife is expecting their second baby. He hopes it is a boy, so he can name him after himself.

Because he left home to work in Pennsylvania, Sanchez's wife and daughter are able to wear new clothes and shoes, live in a nice house in Mexico, and watch television in color. They never have a shortage of food. Los Campos has no major industry, so many residents leave to work in bigger Mexican cities or in the United States.

Sanchez would like eventually to bring his wife and daughter to live with him while he works in Pennsylvania. But the immigration process is slow and tedious. He still is not sure if he wants to stay in the United States. He misses his wife and daughter most of the year. But his dollar bills can buy a lot more in Mexico.

On this day, he looks around at the tall evergreen trees. He takes off his cap and inhales deeply.

"I love the farm," he said. "Farms and the outdoors are all I have known. I don't like boring jobs, like in factories where you have to be in the same spot all day."

Juan de la Rosa, also from Los Campos, trims a tree nearby, giving it a triangular look. That is how Americans like their Christmas trees, he says, in the shape of a triangle.

De la Rosa misses a tall branch, and Sanchez notices. He walks closer and puts his hand on de la Rosa's shoulder.

"You missed that on top," Sanchez says. "It's sticking out."

He cuts the tall branch with a giant pair of clippers. "Like this, OK?"

Over the last decade or so, Sanchez has become the leader of many of the Latino farm workers here. But he does not like the title "foreman." That makes it sound as if he is better or has a higher position than the rest of them.

"We are all the same and do the same job," Sanchez says. "I am the one who speaks more English and knows how to do the job, so the bosses ask me to keep an eye on them. That's all."

In a nearby field, Sanchez hears a familiar voice singing. He chuckles. That must be Abelardo Lopez, he says.

Lopez does not shy away from demonstrating his vocal cords. "With money or without money, I do whatever I want," Lopez sings. "I have no throne or queen, but I am still the king!"

Some of the workers shout and clap, encouraging him when they hear him sing "Y siguo siendo el rey" (And I Am Still the King), a song by the late singer-songwriter Jose Alfredo Jimenez.

Another worker interrupts Lopez's performance: "Let's go to the next row, guys!"

"Que?" (What?) Lopez shouts back.

"Next row!"

Quitting time is 3:00 p.m. At 2:59, the forty or so workers walk toward the company bus that will take them back to their vehicles. Many have backaches, and their hands and arms are sore from raising them above their heads to reach the top branches. Their clothes are stained with sweat and they are hungry. Sanchez needs to drive his friends back to Shenandoah and then drive to where he lives, about ten miles away.

Usually, after work, de la Rosa cooks for himself and the three others who share the three-bedroom, two-story home with him on South Chestnut Street in Shenandoah. Lopez buys a few beers at the corner store, "pa' lo cansado" (to ease their tiredness), he says.

The men sit on a couch and chairs. They do not have a television. But they do have an older boom box that is missing some buttons. "It may be old, but still plays," Lopez says.

They do not have an air conditioner. They open the windows and take their shirts off. It is so hot, they tell each other. They play their music and begin playing a game of cards to kill time and forget about their sore backs.

Most of them look forward to December, when they return home for two months and get to spend some of the money they've earned. They'll wear American brands and the single guys will have lines of girls wanting to go out with them.

"I know it's because of the greens, the dollars," Lopez says jokingly.

They could go outside and enjoy the sun, but on this night they choose to stay inside. At least once a week, they go to the nearby Chinese restaurant for its buffet, and they shop at the grocery store within walking distance or visit a bar on weekends.

They wish they could drive to nearby malls or to the movies. Many of them dream of visiting New York, which they have only seen in movies. But they do not have a car. Their only transportation is the minibus Sanchez drives to take them to the fields.

Lopez offers Sanchez a beer. He declines. He has to drive back home, but he tells Lopez he wants to stay awhile longer. Sanchez sits back and looks out the window. He smiles.

This house is where he finds solace and acceptance. These are the people who understand him the most.

"They are all the people I need when I am here, in the United States," he says. "I'm not alone. They are my family here."

5

LITTLE HERO

To those who don't know second-grader David DeJesus Jr., he looks like a quiet youngster. But behind the angel face is a brave boy who had to grow up faster than most children will, because he lives in one of the poorest neighborhoods of the Lehigh Valley.

His mother, Sandra DeJesus, still in her twenties, calls him a tough little man. To his siblings, he's a hero. David earned his status as a hero a cold November night in 2001, at his house in the 400 block of Tilghman Street, the heart of downtown Allentown. Ever since that night he has walked around his house with his chin up high. Sometimes he sees imaginary evil men and he throws punches and kicks into the air, making a mean face like a professional wrestler. But his mother knows that evil people are not just in his imagination. They abound in their center-city Allentown neighborhood.

"You think it would hurt if I punch the wall?" he asks. He punches the wall of his living room. "It does not!"

His knuckles look a little red. He caresses them gently, trying not be seen by his siblings and two visitors.

"I am the man of the house," he says proudly, placing his hands on his waist, imitating a picture of Batman on a videotape lying on the living room floor.

David took that responsibility seriously when he had to defend his sister, who was eleven years old at the time. He forced her knife-wielding attacker to flee the house. The police arrested a man named Robert Flowers after the incident.

A week later, the family had to relive the attack when Sandra DeJesus, her daughter, and David Jr. attended a court hearing to make sure "that man spends a lot of time in jail," Sandra DeJesus says.

Flowers, who police believe has been involved in similar incidents, was eventually charged with criminal attempt at rape, burglary, criminal trespass, aggravated assault, and simple assault. It was not the fist time he had attacked a young girl in this neighborhood.

For the family, the break-in, no matter how much time passes, remains fresh in their minds. But they have gone back to normal, as much as they can. Sandra would like to move out, to escape the bad memories. But she knows it's not easy. She can't afford to pay rent in suburbia.

That November 6 began like a normal Tuesday for the family of five. The children came home from school, finished their homework, and watched a Disney movie. By 8:30 p.m., David's sister went to bed in the only bedroom in the house. The two boys and the youngest girl followed her. Sandra stayed up until 11 p.m. to wash dishes. "When the kids go to bed, that is the only quiet moment I have for myself," Sandra said.

The quiet did not last long. Sandra was asleep in the living room sometime after 2 a.m. when a man climbed through a window and walked into her kitchen. He grabbed a knife and headed to the bedroom where her children slept. Sandra leaves the bedroom door open so she can hear if the children have nightmares.

The intruder entered and closed the door.

He approached David's sister and put his knees on her legs. He then whispered some words and she awoke, confused.

"I thought it was all a nightmare," she said. "I did not think it was real."

She began screaming, "Mommy! Mommy!" and Sandra woke up to see the bedroom door closed. Sandra knew something was wrong.

David saw his sister trying to get away from the man. He jumped out of bed and punched him in the face four times. He punches out into the air as he retells the story. He then stood between the attacker and his two younger siblings, Joavon and Julissa.

The attacker opened the door to find a frantic mother standing just outside. He punched Sandra and ran away.

Police officers arrested Flowers later that night.

Sandra asks herself what could she have done to prevent her daughter from going through such a traumatic experience.

"I had seen the man roaming the streets," she says. "He knew he could prey on us. How can a person do such a thing?"

David's sister tries to leave the bad experience behind and focus on her future. "I want to be a nurse, doctor, or math teacher," she says.

But Sandra knows her children have lost some of their innocence. The girl and the two youngest ones have the most difficult time going to sleep.

They ask David or their mother to stay near them. They also have nightmares. One night, the youngest dreamed a man stabbed her mother. The little girl woke up and checked under her mother's shirt to make sure she was not cut.

The two little ones call their older brother a hero and say they feel safe near him. They go play outside when he goes to play outside, and they go to bed when he goes to bed.

Joavon tries to imitate his brother's kicks and punches, but David is too fast for him. Joavon says that his brother should be thinking about a cool name for a superhero.

"Spiderman," he says out loud.

David says no. He will think of something better.

"I was not that scared," David says. "I am a superhero."

6

MUSIC TO THEIR EARS

Frances Escalera is feeling somewhat defiant as she turns up the volume slightly on her sixty-inch television set—making it loud enough, she says, for her four children, from toddlers to first-graders, to hear cartoons as they eat their cereal.

"This is America, and this is my house," she says. "They are not telling me how to live in my house."

Turning up the volume on her television and stereo has gotten Escalera into trouble. She and her children face eviction from their center-city apartment.

Three strikes. She's out.

An Allentown ordinance limits how loudly Escalera and other renters, especially in center city, may play their stereos and televisions. If a renter is cited three times in a year for "disruptive conduct"—loud music, rowdy arguments, too much trash— the landlord must evict that renter or risk losing his or her city license to rent.

"What kind of law is this?" asks Escalera.

The law is discriminatory, some city activists agree, because it doesn't take cultural differences into account. This is just another example of a "middle American" town trying to adjust to newcomers with different cultures.

"The law targets people who tend to listen to their music a little loud," says David Vaida, a well-known Allentown lawyer. "We know who they are: Latinos." City officials and some community leaders, however, credit the ordinance with lowering the noise in some neighborhoods.

Many Latinos don't understand the disruptive conduct ordinance or how some of their behavior can be considered disruptive, Vaida and others argue. Playing upbeat, fast-paced music day or night is not uncommon. With center city heavily populated by Latinos living in row houses with thin walls, more of the citations go to them.

Since the 1980s, Allentown has seen an influx of Latinos, who now make up more than a quarter of the city's population. Only one-third of Allentown's Latinos own their homes; the rest are renters.

"The law may not have been created to go after any particular ethnic group," Vaida says. "But it is."

Ever since the law was created in 2000, the majority of citations have gone to Latinos. That's according to the city's Community Development Department.

But the city says the ordinance targets disruptive tenants, regardless of their ethnicity.

Under the older city noise ordinance, fines up to $1,000 can be levied against homeowners, business owners, and renters who cause noise above certain levels. Thresholds vary, depending on whether the noise occurs in residential, business, or government zones.

The disruptive conduct ordinance does not set decibel levels for noise. Police officers are asked to use their judgment to identify conduct that disturbs people in the peaceful enjoyment of their houses. The ordinance is a part of the rental unit licensing law, which is aimed at making landlords responsible for keeping their properties in good condition and evicting problem tenants.

Disruptive conduct is defined as "conduct, action, incident, or behavior perpetrated, caused, or permitted by any occupant or visitor of a residential unit that is so loud, untimely (as to hour of the day), offensive, riotous, or that otherwise disturbs other persons of reasonable sensibility in their personal enjoyment of their premises. It is not necessary that such conduct constitute a criminal offense."

The majority of those cited don't usually repeat the offense, according to City Hall records. But if a person receives three disruptive conduct notices in a year, he or she faces eviction. The person can challenge a citation before an appeals board consisting of seven city employees and community residents.

In July 2001, Escalera appeared before the Disruptive Conduct Board of Appeals, which meets at City Hall. Escalera had been cited for playing music too loudly on her stereo or television set three times within a three-month period. Two other people in similar situations address the board first.

Escalera watches them give their side of the story. Each says their music had not been loud at all. But the officers who had issued the citations said that they could hear the music standing outside the homes, with the doors shut. The board denies both appeals, giving those cited a month to find a new place to live and advising them to keep their noise levels down.

Escalera feels nervous and hopes she will not face the same fate. She walks to the seat assigned for those facing eviction. As she makes her way over, she tells herself she didn't think that she had done anything wrong. In her native Puerto Rico, she tells herself, people tend to listen to music loud. Neighbors are more accepting.

Her name is called. Escalera smiles slightly, trying to hide her nervousness.

Police officer John Guido goes first. He speaks to the board, trying to avoid eye contact with Escalera. He tells the board that he responded to a neighbor's complaint about loud noise in the 400 block of North Church Street. He says he was able to hear the music from a few feet outside her door.

At the time, Escalera wouldn't give the officer her name, but she turned down the volume of her music.

"OK, so I have a big entertainment system," Escalera tells board members. She explains that she owns a big-screen TV, with speakers in different parts of the house.

"I like all kinds of music. Salsa, Spanish music, and hip-hop. Some have bad words with the 'b' and the 'f' and maybe that is why that lady called to complain," she says for simplicity's sake.

Some board members chuckled. She looks confused.

"It is not about the quality of the language," replies Neal Kern, one of the board members. "We all have a different taste in music. This is about you having the music loud that disrupts the peace of others."

The questions ended. Within seconds, the board denies her appeal. Escalera asks if she can challenge the board's decision. She can, in Lehigh County Court. Escalera leaves upset, murmuring some words in Spanish and promising to take her claim to court.

After the hearing, board member Sharon Fraser-Thomas, a member of a local organization called the Alliance for Building Communities, expresses concern for Escalera and her children.

"We are talking about kids and families moving," she says, shaking her head. "Sometimes I don't think this is fair. Some laws are meant to be changed."

Some activists say one person evicted is one too many. Vaida, the lawyer, maintains that the city ordinance should be considered unconstitutional because police officers do not have to measure sound levels to identify disruptive behavior. "There is no objective way to measure what is disruptive," Vaida says. He has taken his argument to Lehigh County Court on behalf of clients who faced eviction but has lost the appeals.

The city says that police officers are given the freedom to judge for themselves. Depending on the location or how many people live near the renter's house, the definition of disruptive conduct may change.

Jose Molina, a former member of the Disruptive Conduct Board and now a critic of the ordinance, says that people who have received three citations are not sure what constitutes being loud or disruptive. What seems sensible to them, he says, may be considered too loud to someone else.

"This law is too vague," Molina says.

Many people who came before the Disruptive Conduct Board when he served were not clear about the ordinance or the penalties it carried.

"I saw a lot of language barriers. Often, the board would be running around City Hall looking for a Spanish speaker. I saw a lot of confusion."

Civic leaders who pushed for the citywide initiative passed by voters said the rental-unit licensing law has brought order to the rental community in Allentown.

Before the law was passed, many landlords did not keep their premises up to standards, forcing renters to live in poor conditions, says Tom Burke, who led the grassroots efforts to pass the law, and other members of the Rental Inspection Committee. He became elected as councilman and served until 2005.

During the first eighteen months of the law, more than 120 units were tagged unfit for human habitation or found to be illegal conversions, remembers Burke.

That proves that the process is working, he says. Landlords are keeping their properties in livable condition, and property values are improving. Committee members also defend the disruptive conduct ordinance that is part of the law.

"People have to get up in the morning, but they can't do that if a neighbor has the music too loud," Burke says. "When you live in an apartment or row house, you don't live alone and have to be respectful of other people who live in the same building or block. We want people to enjoy their homes."

Julio Guridy, who also won a council seat, says that he will work to keep the noise level down in the city. Even he has problems going to sleep at night because of rowdy neighbors near his Fourteenth Street home, he says. But perhaps eviction is a big punishment, he reflects.

Three Strikes

A few days after facing the eviction board, Escalera begins packing her belongings and looking for a new place to live.

She thought about gathering everybody she knew and marching in front of City Hall to "stop that law." But she could not garner enough support among her neighbors.

Instead, she found lawyer Lori Molloy of Lehigh Valley Legal Services, a non-profit organization for low-income people seeking legal representation. Molloy, who filed an appeal to Lehigh County Court, argues that the ordinance does not provide an objective way to measure whether Escalera was disruptive in playing music.

"I am not giving up so easily," Escalera says. She will leave the apartment, because she has to. But she will continue expressing her discontent over the law. After all, she says, people in center city are at a disadvantage over other Allentonians, because they live in row houses and it's easier to hear neighbors arguing and playing music.

"I just can't believe it," Escalera says, covering her face with both hands. It's hard to accept that she has to find a new house and move her children to a new school. "All because, what? Some neighbors say I play my television too loud?"

Escalera's next-door neighbor, Janet Corado, also faced eviction after receiving three citations for loud music.

"Loud music is running people out of their houses," Corado says. "It is silly."

Corado appealed her eviction to the Disruptive Conduct Board and lost. She then appealed to a district magistrate. Her landlord testified on her behalf, saying that he was willing to keep her as a tenant. Magistrate Diane Jepsen ruled in 2001 that she could stay.

Still, Corado moved a few weeks later to a less expensive apartment.

"I just wanted to show the city that what they did was not right," Corado said. "Other people should challenge too."

7

PRICELESS

Wedding consultant Kathleen Arey isn't Puerto Rican, but she knows all about Puerto Rican customs and other Latino celebrations, such as quinceañeras, which mark a girl's fifteenth birthday and her transition into womanhood.

Such knowledge is more than a passing interest for Arey. It's business. More than 40 percent of her customers at David's Bridal in Whitehall Township, just a few miles from Allentown, are of Puerto Rican or other Latino descent, and they come to buy dresses for weddings, quinceañeras, and other special occasions. "And they keep coming," she said.

Like Arey, other business owners are recognizing a growing truth in the Lehigh Valley: Puerto Ricans and other Latinos have money to spend. They spend it at local supermarkets, clothing shops, car dealerships, and many other places. And as they increase in number in the region, so does their collective buying power.

"Hispanics are growing faster than the rest of the population," said Sue Sampson, spokeswoman for State Farm Insurance in Allentown. "It only makes sense to reach them now.

"I have a feeling that more and more businesses will come to the realization that they cannot continue doing business and ignore 24, 25, or 30 percent of the population," she said.

Puerto Ricans are the dominant Latino market segment (and 60 percent of the Latino population) in the Lehigh Valley and surrounding six counties, according to most recent census figures. Most reside in Allentown, where they are close to 70 percent of the Latino population, and in Bethlehem, where they are close to 80 percent of the Latino population.

In the region, Puerto Ricans are nearly 3 percent of total population, but they are about a quarter of the total population in Allentown and 14 percent of the total population in Bethlehem—and the numbers are growing.

National chains have already recognized the importance of Latino buying power (income available to spend after paying for essentials such as food and housing). The Selig Center for Economic Growth at the University of Georgia puts Latino buying power at more than $450 billion nationally.

To reach the market, McDonald's, Kraft Foods, Budweiser, and other companies advertise on the Spanish-language networks Univision and Telemundo, carried on

Lehigh Valley cable systems. Local businesses advertise in Spanish-language news-papers and on the radio, hire bilingual staff, and print literature in Spanish.

"It is important to have a relationship with the Latino community," said Pedro Rubio, a MAC Mortgage loan officer in Allentown. "It's a growing market. It's common sense."

Lissette Rivera, who was born in Puerto Rico and lives in Bethlehem, started a venture to take advantage of the local Latino buying power in the summer of 2002. Her "Hispanic Discount Card," which she sells for $20, offers cardholders dis-counts from businesses that have signed up for the program. In turn, the busi-nesses are marketed in Latino neighborhoods. Non-Latinos also can buy the card.

"I just ask them [local businesses] if they want to increase their number of Latino customers, and they all say, 'Yes,'" Rivera said. "I don't have to do much negotiation."

The business owners pay no fees to Rivera. She makes her profit on sales of the card.

Steve Mohle, who owns Regal Furniture in Bethlehem, signed on the moment Rivera told him about the card idea. Mohle said he only had to spend a few min-utes talking to Rivera to know that he was making the right decision. In the past few years, he has seen a steady stream of Latino customers.

"We attract all customers, of any ethnicity," Mohle said. "We realize that His-panics are big in the local market."

Businesses can better court Latino customers if they better understand their traditions and buying habits.

Latinos depend on Spanish-language radio and television for information and entertainment, said Nestor Velazquez, who owns WNV Advertising in Allentown with his wife, Wanda. "So, that's the best way to get them."

Visibility usually pays off.

"You have to be in the Latino parade, in the events where you know there are going to be a lot of Latinos. It makes no sense to advertise on television if all of the Latinos are out watching the parade."

Also, a large number of Latino families consist of not only parents and children but also extended family members living in the same house or on the same block. Latino women ages eighteen to forty-nine tend to shop for three or more family members, according to research by WNV Advertising.

"Once you get her, you get the husband, kids, *tia* [aunt], *abuelita* [grandmother], the whole family," Velazquez said.

For Carmen Garcia, of Allentown, it is customary in places such as her native Puerto Rico for the woman of the house to buy the clothes and groceries for the entire family. Her mother before her did, and her married daughters do the same in their own homes.

"My husband only shops when I give him a list," said Garcia, in her forties, after shopping at the Little Apple Market in the heart of downtown Allentown. "And even then, I have to write everything in detail. It's the only way we know."

She spends most of the family money on groceries. They prefer to eat in, rather than eat out. She likes to shop at stores that cater to Latinos and that sell products from Puerto Rico and other Latin American countries. "I see more stores selling Latin products," she said. "But more of them would be good."

Alex Ortiz, in his mid-twenties, also a Puerto Rican native, listens to advertisements in both Spanish and English. But those with a Latin theme, in either language, tend to catch his attention.

"I just buy stuff I need, like food and clothes," said Ortiz, who lives alone and tends to do all of his own shopping. "I like to buy where I know they like Latinos."

Several factors make Latinos attractive consumers. Although they tend to earn less than Americans as a whole, Latinos in America also tend to invest less and save less money a year, according to the Association of Hispanic Advertising Agencies in McLean, Virginia.

"This means that Latinos have more disposable cash a year than other ethnic groups," Velazquez said.

Also, Latinos are among the youngest populations in the United States. Their average age is twenty-six, compared to an average age of thirty-four for non-Latinos, according to the U.S. Census figures. They are at the peak of their consumption years, shopping for new jobs, cars, rental properties, and houses, according to research by La Mega Communications, a twenty-four-hour Spanish-language radio station at channel 1320 AM.

Since many Puerto Ricans moved to the Valley in the last decade, businesses have an opportunity to cultivate a loyalty to their brands, said Ed Macias, former director of La Mega.

The Lehigh Valley Chamber of Commerce organizes workshops to educate members about Latino buying patterns.

State Farm Insurance officials have sponsored "mixers," or gatherings for Latino business and community leaders, and have translated their Web site information and literature into Spanish so that language is not a barrier for prospective customers.

Most Puerto Ricans and other Latinos in the Valley are working class, pointed out economist Kamran Afshar. As they move into higher-paying jobs to satisfy the need for nurses, bank tellers, and teachers, for example, to serve their growing population, they may lose that market identity.

As ethnic groups become middle class, they tend to speak the language of the community at large and no longer buy ethnic products or subscribe to ethnic media like previous generations, said Afshar, of KAA Inc., a research market company in Bethlehem.

"As any group expands in numbers, so does the interest in that group," Afshar said. "But as groups becomes more affluent, they become less ethnic."

The Irish and the Italians who came to the United States in the late nineteenth and early twentieth centuries are no longer targeted by big companies, he pointed out.

"But," he added, "Latinos are not exactly like other groups. And while we can project there will be similarities to what other groups went through, we have to see."

8

THE FEARFUL SIDE OF BUSINESS

It's a weekday afternoon and Erlinda Agron steps out of her office on the South Side of Bethlehem, the second largest city in the Lehigh Valley.

Her eyes focus on a line of mostly Latino-owned businesses, with few people walking in and out. Other businesses have closed for good. Agron sees potential but knows the challenges of the neighborhood. One is the cultural separation between the Latino business district and its neighbors—mostly white, middle-class Lehigh University students.

Agron has made it her mission to bring together South Side Latinos and the college students, who have money to spend on food and clothes. She is educating each group about the other's needs.

"If the college students were to come here and shop, this place would look more lively," she says. "They are right there, a few blocks away."

She also wants to reach out to other shoppers who visit center city but seldom make their way across the Fahy Bridge into the South Side's ethnic enclave.

"Many people just make assumptions. They are going by the bad news they hear," Agron says, referring to crime stories that focus on Latinos as perpetrators. "When something bad happens, everybody talks about it. Not everything is wonderful in the South Side, but there are many good things."

In many cities like Bethlehem and Allentown, Latinos tend to form their own *barrio*, or neighborhood, where they feel comfortable, speak Spanish, and buy products of their home countries.

But the problem comes when Latinos become isolated from the rest of the city and receive fewer resources as a result, said Raul Yzaguirre, president of the National Council of La Raza, the nation's largest Hispanic organization.

The latest U.S. Census numbers showed that Latinos in Bethlehem tend to live in the same neighborhoods. The eastern portion of the South Side is predominantly Latino.

Agron became head of the Community Action Development Committee (CADC) in 2002. Since then, Agron and her small staff created a series of programs to better market the area to what she calls "outsiders." The CADC of the Lehigh Valley is a private, nonprofit agency, funded by donations and government grants, whose mission is to revitalize urban areas.

Agron has organized workshops to educate business owners about credit card fraud and personal safety and to help them create flyers and business cards to boost sales. She advised owners to post their hours of operation and told them to consider remodeling their facades.

She also started tours to familiarize high school students with the ethnic enclave and is reaching out to Lehigh University students.

Always a People Person

Agron's efforts to help bring people together started long before she arrived in Bethlehem. She spent much of her teen years as a volunteer, helping civil war victims in her native El Salvador.

She moved to Allentown in 1992 and received bachelor's and master's degrees in economics from Moravian College, often taking her three sons with her to class when she could not find a babysitter. She became a member of the Latin Alliance, a volunteer advocacy group that works on Latino issues. She became president in 2000.

"One cannot just wake one day and decide to make a difference," she said. "You have to be well prepared and know what you are talking about."

Agron became more interested in the empty South Side when the city of Bethlehem released a report in the summer of 2002. There was something mysterious about the content, she remembered.

"We were mysteriously forgotten," she said.

The study assessed the needs of the historical section of the South Side—about ninety acres bordering Second, Taylor, and Morton streets. But the section where Latinos operate their businesses, the 700 block of East Fourth Street, and the surrounding businesses were not included.

Tony Hanna, the city's director of community and economic development at the time, said the east end was not included because the city did not have enough money to include all of the South Side.

A second study, led by the CADC, quickly followed and focused on the east end, "the second South Side downtown," Hanna said.

The second study found that the second portion of the South Side needed more playgrounds, senior and youth centers, and other programs. Once the city expressed willingness to recognize the second study, Agron got to work to bring more people to the area.

She contacted area high schools and arranged for students to check out ethnic restaurants, stores, and other sites.

"Maybe they will go back to their parents and friends and will say, 'Mom, Dad, there is this neat Caribbean restaurant in the South Side and is not so bad,' and they will bring more people over," she said.

Then, Agron went after Lehigh University students with the approval of Thomas Hyclak, an economics professor and chairman of the economics department at Lehigh.

A group of twenty college students surveyed their peers and found that many thought the fronts of the businesses looked like homes. They also noticed that most shops did not post hours of operation or the services or goods they sell.

To attract the students, business owners need to advertise in the university newspaper and distribute flyers on campus, the students found. But mostly, the students found that their peers were afraid of the unknown. After 6 p.m., streets in the eastern section are dark because there are few streetlights.

"Students do not want to walk out in the dark," said George Stavovcik, the CADC's business development director at the time.

Lindsey Carloni, a Lehigh University student involved in the survey, said some of her classmates thought "it was a little scary" to walk there on their own.

Bethlehem Police Commissioner Francis Donchez Jr. said that there is more police presence on the South Side because it's more heavily populated than other parts of town. People tend to live in row houses and apartments.

"When you have more people in concentrated areas, you are going to have more crime," Donchez said. "But I cannot say it's out of control."

Of the crime issue, he said, "I think it's mostly a perception, but a perception does not mean it's true."

Once the Lehigh students talked to some of the business owners, Carloni understood why some do not have time to advertise or decorate their storefronts.

"Some of them work one or two jobs besides owning a business," she said. "I had no idea of that before I went there."

It will take time to eliminate cultural barriers, Hyclak said.

"Students do not shop here," he said. "They go to the malls and fast-food restaurants. They go to suburbia."

Agron, though determined, admits that changes come slowly.

"It's like going through a checklist," she said, adding that making both groups aware of each other's needs is progress. "Once you have accomplished one goal, then you go to the next."

9

SIDE BY SIDE

Teenagers Dania Liz Gonzalez and Alexis Matias are proud to be Puerto Rican. But the two girls are as different as a San Juan beach and a New York streetscape. Dania speaks mostly Spanish, and when she speaks English, it's with an accent. She wears bright colors, mostly dresses, jeans, and T-shirts. She likes *tostones*—fried slices of plantain and rice and beans—as well as the quick rhythm of salsa music. If she closes her eyes, she can hear the singing of birds in her native Puerto Rico and the crash of waves on its shores.

Alexis speaks mostly English. She likes to wear bandanas, tight jeans, and T-shirts that show her belly. She thinks tostones and rice and beans are OK, but she likes pizza and hamburgers better. She has never been fond of salsa music and listens instead to hip-hop and pop.

A native New Yorker, Alexis has never been to Puerto Rico, but knows it is an island somewhere in the Caribbean.

Dania and Alexis—one an islander, the other a mainlander—are part of the mix that is the Puerto Rican community in the Lehigh Valley and the rest of the United States.

For decades, the majority of Puerto Ricans in the Valley had come directly from rural Puerto Rico. But since the early 1980s, Puerto Ricans born in New York and New Jersey have begun to move to the Valley in larger numbers. And many of Puerto Rican descent have been born here.

Though Dania and Alexis live distinct lifestyles, they know each other and cross paths at events that promote Puerto Rican culture. In dance and music, each can demonstrate what it means to her to be Puerto Rican.

Dania Liz Gonzalez

When Dania Liz Gonzalez moved from Caguas, Puerto Rico, to Allentown with her family, she thought she'd fit in easily. After all, almost half of the students at William Allen High School are Latino, most of them of Puerto Rican descent.

"Well, it did not happen like I thought," Dania says.

She quickly learned that many of those who are Puerto Rican identified more with being "Nuyorican"—second-generation Puerto Ricans born in New York or other states who are more in tune with the American way of life.

The term Nuyorican is commonly used by island-born Puerto Ricans to describe Puerto Ricans from New York. Second-generation Puerto Ricans born on the mainland have also adopted the term to describe themselves. Spelling variations include "Neorican" and "New Yorrican."

"Nuyo what?" was Dania's reaction when she first learned why she dressed and spoke differently from other Puerto Ricans in the Valley.

Dania found it difficult to make friends with Puerto Ricans born on the mainland because they had little in common.

She feels closer to new arrivals from Latin American countries. She met her best friend, a native of the Dominican Republic, in an English for Speakers of Other Languages (ESOL) class, where newcomers learn English. "She is not Puerto Rican, but our cultures are so much alike," Dania says.

Dania's cousin, Jose Sola, moved to the Lehigh Valley from Puerto Rico around the same time she did, but made an easier transition. Dania observed that Sola used to wear clothes that fit him "just right." Nowadays, he wears baggy T-shirts and jeans, listens to some English music, and hangs out with Puerto Rican students born here.

"I can't do that," she says. "That's like, not from the Puerto Rico I know." Dania has embraced the Puerto Rican community here, though. She is active in the Puerto Rico Cultural Alliance in Allentown, which annually sponsors the Puerto Rican Day Parade in the city. In fact, she was parade queen in 2001. She used the spotlight to encourage other Puerto Rican girls to honor their roots—specifically not to try to look skinny because of the influence of American television and magazines.

"I am not a skinny girl and when I won for queen, I just thought, 'Good, now I can show other girls who are not skinny that they too can become queens,'" she says. "I am just the way I was in Puerto Rico and I am not going to change just because I live here."

Alexis Matias

Alexis Matias was born in Brooklyn, New York. She remembers how her grandfather would play salsa music almost every day when she was a child. But when she went outside to play, she heard other children speaking English, not Spanish, or a combination of Spanish and English. And the youngsters would sing along to English-language songs.

At age seven, she moved to Bethlehem with her family. There, she watched MTV and listened to bands like TLC, a hip-hop/pop trio, and more recently, Jennifer Lopez.

She has only seen Puerto Rico in pictures.

Still, her father has made sure she knows her heritage. He still talks about *la isla del encanto*—the enchanted islands many Puerto Ricans call Puerto Rico.

"I am Puerto Rican," Alexis says. "That's what I am."

Many of Alexis's friends at Liberty High School in nearby Bethlehem—Shamara Nickens, Casandra Clark, and Sandra Troche, for example, all in their early teens—have never been to Puerto Rico either. They share the same passion for rap and hip-hop music.

They can tell if other Puerto Ricans are islanders by the way they dress and the music they listen to.

"They like Spanish music, like salsa and merengue, and, oh, *bachata*," says her friend Troche. "That's too slow for us. Bachata is, like, slow Puerto Rican ballads."

Together

Dania and Alexis came together when a local group called the Puerto Rican Cultural Alliance sponsored a talent show at St. John's Lutheran Church in downtown Allentown.

Before their performances, Alexis and her friends rehearse their dance steps to the hit "For My People" by Missy Elliot.

In a nearby room, Dania practices the lyrics of the salsa song, "Me Canse," which she will lip-sync.

When the curtain opens, Alexis and her friends adjust their bandanas and walk on stage. With hip-hop blasting for their performance, the girls jump and express themselves with their hands as they bound about the stage.

People in the audience cheer and clap.

A few minutes later, Dania walks to the stage and performs her song about a woman who is tired of being in a love triangle. She stays in the same spot, but moves her legs to the rhythm of the fast-paced salsa.

Adults in the audience recognize the lyrics, and some sing along. Later, Dania dances to a traditional Puerto Rican song with other high school–aged girls and boys.

When the show is over, Dania and Alexis stand side by side in front of a huge Puerto Rican flag and embrace each other. Both look at each other and smile, their first encounter. But their friendship does not go beyond a friendly smile. The crowd cheers. Dania, still wearing her traditional Puerto Rican dress, stands on the right; Alexis, on the left.

"¡Arriba Puerto Rico!" (Long live Puerto Rico!) somebody in the audience yells.

BLATINOS

Elsa Vazquez remembers being eight years old and running to her mother, excited about buying her first headband, a yellow one.

"Why did you buy such a bright color?" her mother asked. The yellow will contrast with your skin color and more people will notice you are black, her mother told her.

Vazquez, who was living in the Dominican Republic at the time, looked at her skin. She was black indeed. She headed back to the store to return the headband and buy a black one, to match her skin color.

That was the day Vazquez, now in her late forties and living in Allentown, became conscious of her identity. And ever since, she has learned to live with a dual identity, that of being black and Latino.

"I feel comfortable in a room with people of color," she said.

Some black Latinos say the dual identities present challenges because they do not feel part of any particular group. They struggle to honor their African roots, but also try to display their loyalty to countries such as the Dominican Republic, Colombia, and Puerto Rico.

"A lot of people don't understand the mixture of Latino, African, Indian, Spaniard," Allentown resident Juan Orta said. "There is no one Latino look. I look black, and I am black. But I am also a proud Puerto Rican."

Some say there are Latinos who see them as black and not part of their ethnic circle. There are also some African Americans who see them as Latinos and do not consider skin color to be enough to welcome them into the black community.

They are simply the reflection of the diversity among the Latino community. Many of the Latinos from the Caribbean islands can trace their ancestors to Africa. Beginning in the 1500s, the slave trade took Africans to several parts of Latin America.

Over the centuries they assimilated into different cultures; some mixed with Europeans and natives.

Vazquez inherited her black skin from her father, who traces his ethnicity to Haiti. She was raised by her mother, a fair-skinned Dominican, and her relatives.

"I was the only black one in the family," she said.

In her office, Vazquez keeps a collection of eight black dolls by her desk to remind her of her roots. She is a social worker at St. Luke's Hospital in Fountain Hill, in a town just a few miles southeast of Allentown.

"I like them," she said. "As a child, I only played with black dolls, because they looked like me."

Orta, a native of Puerto Rico, shares similar values. He and his family embrace both cultures—the Latino side, with his Puerto Rican roots, and his African side.

At reunions, family members play Africanlike drums with a combination of Latino salsa and soul lyrics.

"A lot of people are surprised to learn that I am Puerto Rican because of my features," Orta said. "I don't have a double personality. I just accept where I come from."

Orta traces his African roots to his father's side of the family. His father, who still lives in Puerto Rico, and his aunt have always worn African-style clothing, he said. His father usually wears long white shirts and pants, and his aunt always preferred bright-colored dresses, wraps on her head, and big earrings, he said.

His father gave him a *pango*, an African drum made out of hollow wood and rabbit skin. He plays it at home and at events to showcase part of his culture, he said.

"If you try to be who you are not, you are confusing your children," he said of the importance of teaching youth about mixed racial identity.

Kevin Castro, in his thirties, says that he also has developed a "thick skin" over the years here in Bethlehem. When he speaks in English, people assume he is African American. When he speaks Spanish, some people are surprised.

Well, of course, he says. He is a native of Colombia.

"I am 100 percent Hispanic, and African American by adoption," he said. "I am of African descent, but I am Latino."

Castro noticed he was different from other Latinos—his skin was darker—when he was about five years old and living in Colombia. When he moved to Miami a few years later, his African American friends noticed that he did not share a similar taste in music and clothes and thought he acted "too white," he said.

Among Latinos, he often felt conscious about his skin color. When a friend invited him to a religious event at her house, he asked if "they would welcome black people."

Sure, his friend replied, explaining that the church had a lot of black members.

But most of that was in the past, he said. Today, like Orta and Vazquez, he is proud to be a black Latino. The combination makes him a more interesting person, he says.

Yet every now and then, he faces a sense of separation, a sense that he is not fully Latino.

"Sometimes I hear some Latinos talking bad about black people and then they look at me and say 'Oh, not you, the other black people,'" he said. "That aggravates me."

Some black Latinos say that sharing more than one race or culture often leads them to learn more about their ancestry. They appreciate the history and culture of Africa and at the same time display their Latino pride.

"We are more exotic," Vazquez said.

JULIO

From a distance it could be easy to miss Julio Guridy. He sits at the very end of the council chamber, to the right. He is short, so a person in the back seat at a crowded council meeting would have to stand up to see him and connect the voice with the man, the only one with an accent here.

But make no mistake, Julio's personality and character are hard to miss—at five foot six. He is the first Latino immigrant to get elected to the Allentown City Council, a task that seemed almost impossible when he arrived here in the 1970s, a time when racism in many small American cities was rampant. These days Julio Guridy can be seen frequently on television news, both in Spanish and English, in the pages of the local newspaper, at important civic functions, and at local and state government gatherings.

"Ah, Julio lo veo hasta en la sopa" (I see him even in my soup), says Myra Denisse Pina, a medical activist, using a common expression from the Dominican Republic, the country to which both trace their heritage. Pina met Guridy ten years ago, when both had become interested in helping Latinos and joined several nonprofit organizations. Guridy whispered to her then that he dreamed of getting into government.

"I remember thinking, 'You don't know what's going on,'" she says, referring to Guridy's hope of holding elected office. "A Latino in government? In Allentown?"

Later, she moved to Italy for several years, and returned in 2004 to see signs everywhere asking voters to reelect Guridy to the city council. Guridy is not a common name among Latinos. She thought, Could it be him?

"I was like, 'Wow, he did it,'" she recalls.

Guridy cannot enter into a room without people whispering to each other, I heard he arrived to this country with $5 in his pocket and look at him now!

While the legend is an exaggeration, it is not that far off either. At age fourteen, Guridy, his mother, stepfather, and two sisters arrived in the Lehigh Valley in January 1975. The family had a total of $5,000 to settle in the new country.

"That's not a lot of money for five people," Guridy says. "Even for back then."

He spoke very little English, so he began taking classes in the sixth grade in Spanish as part of a bilingual program. He kept up with his courses, and little by little, as he learned the language, he began taking some of his classes in English. He proved a fast learner and was promoted to the seventh grade shortly after. By eighth grade he took most of his classes in English.

Seeing potential in the young student, teachers enrolled Guridy in a program for high school freshmen who show promise. He began learning about college and enrollment requirements thanks to East Stroudsburg University's Upward Bound program.

He spent summers during high school taking courses at the university, and because he also needed to chip in at home, he also took a job at his neighborhood Boys & Girls Club, assisting the adults and looking after younger kids.

"Many Latino parents don't talk to their kids about college," he says. "With this program, college became part of my everyday vocabulary and something to plan ahead."

He attended the same university after high school and graduated in 1984 with a bachelor's in sociology and criminal justice and a minor in administration. He then pursued a master's in sociology at Indiana University of Pennsylvania.

"All of which came in handy as a city councilman," he says.

He took jobs at Latino-related organizations and later at an area bank, while getting involved as an activist for Latinos at the same time. He worked to help Latinos open their own businesses through grants. He helped create an organization called Latin Alliance for Latinos Leaders, where Latino leaders meet and discuss ways to improve quality of life for new arrivals. He also opened his own travel business in nearby Bethlehem. But he never forgot his dream to get involved in government.

"As an activist, you do a lot of complaining, but you can't really change much," he says. "As a city lawmaker, I could do that."

He decided to run for office in 1999, when then council member Emma Tropiano was known for associating the city's ills with the growing Latino population. She blamed crime, decreasing property values, dilapidated buildings, and other problems on Latinos. (She died in early 2003.) Her statements appeared frequently in local media, taking her to the city council seat many times. She said what others thought, she used to say. In 1992, she lobbied to implement English as the only official language of the city. It failed.

"People used to believe her. She said what many felt but did not say out loud," he says. "She was in a position of power. I wanted to show that she was not correct."

Guridy campaigned in 1999 and lost. Two years later, with his name on more people's radar, he ran again. He focused on serving as a voice not only for Spanish-speaking Latinos, but also for the population at large.

"If I ran as a Latino candidate only, I would not have won," he says. "One needs to serve for all people."

Guridy won a second seat in 2005. Though the state does not track voters based on race or ethnicity, Guridy speculates that more Latinos went out to vote because they are hungry for people like them in positions of power.

Allentown voters first elected a candidate of Puerto Rican heritage, Marty Velasquez III, in 1993. But most Spanish-speaking Latinos don't approach him because he does not speak Spanish. He is seen more as a symbolic connection between the Pennsylvania Dutch settlers and the new Latino arrivals. His mother is Pennsylvania Dutch. His father is from Puerto Rico.

"People are hungry for someone like them in government," Guridy says. "They see me and want me to solve all of their problems, even their personal ones with their husbands and wives."

However, Guridy does admit that sometimes all of his involvement can get to be a bit much. He would like to see more Latinos taking charge and posting their signs all over town asking for people's votes. There are a few interested, he confides. But maybe one of the new arrivals will surprise him the same way he surprised Myra Denisse Pina.

"I can't be the only one. I can only live for so long," he says jokingly.

COLORFUL PAGES

The Spanish title and the light brown color of the characters' skin on the book's cover are what first caught Jacqueline Rodriguez's attention.

Rodriguez, a young mother in her twenties, liked what she saw on the page: an older Latino woman and a girl holding hands and flying in the air. She liked the title of Arthur Dorros's book *La Isla*, which means island, and began turning the pages to read the content in English.

She was drawn into the story from the get-go. A Latino girl travels with her grandmother from New York City to a Caribbean island for a day to rediscover her roots.

"This is the kind of book I want my daughter to read," Rodriguez, who lives in Allentown, said. "It's hard to find books where my children can read about children who look just like them and speak English."

Like the Rodriguez family, many Lehigh Valley readers are discovering a new selection of books in their local libraries. Libraries in Allentown, Bethlehem, Easton, Emmaus, and elsewhere in the Lehigh Valley are beginning to carry multicultural books—books in English that have minority characters, mostly Latino—to serve their growing Latino communities.

Librarians say their readers are asking for more books about bicultural Latino children living in America—children who live in an English-speaking world but interact with Spanish-speaking parents.

"These books are gaining popularity as more Latinos move into Allentown," said Sharon Frankenfield, head of children's services at the Allentown Public Library. "We have to be aware of the needs of the community, and we try to cater to them."

Frankenfield said that she began seeing a similar trend a few decades ago with more books including African American children in their plots. Now, more bilingual children do not have to look far from their neighborhoods to find the voices of writers who understand them, she said.

"And they are pretty popular, too," said Beth Rosania, former coordinator of youth services at the Bethlehem Public Library. Today, she is the head of the Easton Public Library's youth services. "People who come here are from all backgrounds, and we need to serve them."

Rodriguez brings her children at least twice a week to the library and has grown fascinated with the number of English books with Latino characters, but she said she would like to see even more books like *La Isla.*

As she keeps reading, she remembers her days as a little girl in Brooklyn, New York, living in a Spanish-speaking household.

In the story, the grandmother grabs the little girl's hands and together they fly through the air to an unnamed Caribbean island.

The grandmother takes the little girl to the town square, the outdoor *mercado* (market), and parks. The girl notices that the weather is much hotter, and people smile and talk to each other more often than in the city, and they wear colorful clothes, such as bright orange and pink shirts and shorts.

"It's nice to have some books where our children can see a reflection of themselves," Rodriguez said.

Her children Eliana, a third-grader, and Kenith, a fifth-grader, said they prefer to read books in English that include children their age and their ethnicity and live similar lives.

"I like to read more in English than Spanish," Eliana said, who on this day played computer games at the Allentown Public Library. "It's nice to read about Latino children. I also like space and scary books."

"Books who have kids like me are pretty interesting," Kenith said.

Aracelis Valentin, another young Allentown mother of two, came across multicultural books when she first visited the Allentown Public Library in 2001. She wanted books that would help her children practice their English reading skills while conserving their heritage, she told the librarian.

"They showed me all these wonderful books, and I had to bring some of them home right away," Valentin said in Spanish. "Now, they cannot stop reading them."

Her children Coralis Marquez, a second-grader, and Jonathan Marquez, a third-grader, ask her to take them to the library a few times a week. "I'll do what they want as long as it makes them want to read," she said.

In the past decade, small presses have produced the works of about a dozen Latino writers of children's books. Some readers, like Valentin, hope that more commercial publishers take notice and follow that lead.

Children of other ethnic groups can also benefit from reading books about Latino children by being exposed to a culture they usually see only from a distance. Children from all ethnic, racial, and cultural groups need books that are representative of their own lives and cultures. It's much easier to identify with story characters if the characters look like you, think like you, and act like you, the mothers said. The demand for books about children who live in English and Spanish environments simultaneously is already high at Allentown, Bethlehem, Emmaus, and Easton public libraries, librarians said.

Some of the most popular books include the Josefina series. The books tell the story of a nine-year-old Mexican American girl who lives with her family on a ranch near Santa Fe, New Mexico, in the 1820s. Josefina, her three sisters, and their father try to carry on after the death of their mother.

Many Latino children ask for books written by noted Mexican American author Gary Soto, Frankenfield said. One of his most popular books remains *Too Many Tamales*, which he co-wrote with Ed Martinez. The book tells the story of a girl who insists on helping her mother cook tamales for a Christmas dinner celebration. Maria, the girl, puts her mom's ring on her finger and later drops it into the dough. She realizes that she no longer has the ring on her hand after both are done cooking the tamales. Maria and her three cousins eat all of the tamales, hoping to find the ring before her mother does. At the end of the story, the children discover that the mother had the ring all along.

Johanna Hurwitz's book *Class President*, another favorite, tells the story of a young Latino boy who decides not to run for class president so he can help a friend run his campaign. The boy later struggles with his decision, knowing that he is more qualified for the office than his friend.

Sandra Del Cueto, a Spanish professor at Northampton Community College, said that Latino children need to see many more books like these in area libraries, schools, and homes. "There should be more Latino children represented in books, books that show the world they live in," Del Cueto said. "Children nowadays do not identify themselves with the book characters, and begin thinking they are different from the rest of the world."

Rodriguez read to the end of *La Isla*. She saw glossy pictures of a little girl flying back from a Caribbean island to New York City. The sun had been replaced by the moon, and the open land with the city skyline.

The girl in the story felt more American than ever, but at the same time closer to her Latino roots, by witnessing firsthand how people live and work in the country where her grandmother was born and raised.

"It reminds me of when I was a little girl living in New York City," Rodriguez said. "I want my children to have that same connection, to see themselves in books."

ABCS

The lunch break ends at Raub Middle School and sixth-grader Alexander Londono waits in the back of the line for permission to enter his classroom. Shifting from foot to foot, he sees and hears the tall woman he calls "Missus" as she gives instructions. He cannot understand all of the words.

"(Something) in line," he hears. "(Something), (something) please. (Something) quiet."

Sometimes Alexander, who moved to Allentown from Colombia and is still learning English, wonders if he's missing important information. Unable to understand all of Missus's words, he follows the other children into Room 214.

Missus will teach in English to help Alexander, better known as Alex, and the other students learn the language—an everyday challenge for students enrolled in a program called English for Speakers of Other Languages (ESOL).

"If I knew English," Alex says later in Spanish, "I would be smarter here."

Alex feels alone in this giant English-speaking world. But he does not know that his story reflects the frustrations that many new students face in trying to learn a language while dealing with the everyday pressures of being a preteen or teenager. After all, more than 10 percent of the students in the Allentown School District take ESOL classes. In nearby Bethlehem, the figure is about 8 percent.

As in most schools around the country, in Allentown, middle school ESOL students spend most of the day with one teacher who provides instruction in English in various subjects, including language instruction. Some are in ESOL classes for up to two years, while others move into regular classes more quickly, depending on when they become fluent in English. In high school, students may take one or more ESOL classes, depending on their needs. Educators teach in English but at a slower pace than the regular classes.

Without the personalized attention, ESOL students would not learn or do well in school, educators say.

Allentown's nonnative speakers come from all parts of the world: Latin America, Africa, the Middle East. Often, they are learning English from scratch, trying to catch up to their grade level, make new friends, and learn the system.

As the district grows more diverse, educators are faced with helping newcomers master the language, learn math and other subjects, and perform well in the Pennsylvania System of School Assessment.

"Life is not easy for these students," says Ana Sainz de la Pena, a former ESOL administrator with the Allentown district. "They are pulled from a world familiar to them and dropped into another one completely different."

A poster of a smiling gorilla greets Alex and his classmates, about twenty in all, as they enter the room. Missus—Carmelina Subervi, one of two teachers in Raub's ESOL program—hands back their vocabulary tests. Alex had memorized the spellings. He is anxious to know his grade. He eyes Missus as she makes her way to his desk and hands him back his test.

"Yes!" he says, jumping out of his desk. "Ninety-three!"

He scans the test. The minus sign next to one of the words surprises him.

He did spell "shart" correctly, he says, so why did he get points taken off? He pronounces the word out loud. "Shart." Yes, it sounds right.

"No Missus, si la escribi bien" (I did write it correctly), he says, running out of the English words he knows. Missus smiles, pointing at the paper. He should have used a "k" at the end, not a "t," she tells him.

Alex looks puzzled. He scratches his head.

"You should have used the 'k,' not the 't,'" she says again, speaking slowly, making sure Alex understands every word. "You did good. It's a 93."

"Aaaahh. OK Missus."

The teacher walks to the center of the room to explain how to avoid spelling errors, such as not necessarily spelling words they way they might sound. "Remember," she tells the fifth- and sixth-graders. "Even if you are writing in a different language, you have to follow the rules."

Alex often feels confused about the language and his surroundings. When speaking or writing, he wonders if he used a "c" instead of a "z" in a word. After all, the consonants sound similar. He wonders why "buy" changes to "bought" in the past tense, when the teacher just told him to add "ed" to actions that have already happened.

He wonders if he will ever be able to speak English as fast as the other Raub students.

He wonders, too, about the school rules. Why do students have to form lines to the cafeteria, where a lady gives instructions over a microphone? Many of the words he cannot grasp. She speaks too fast: Sit down now. Don't yell. Stand in line and please leave that girl alone. And the food. He's had better.

School was different in Colombia. He got a lot of 10s, a perfect grade. He understood his teachers, who spoke in Spanish, his first language. And he had beans and rice for lunch. Good food.

But Alex understands that he has a new life with his parents in America and that he must learn the American way.

Usually, a newcomer needs two years to learn basic communication skills, and five to seven years to learn to write and read like a native speaker, experts say. ESOL students, as well as others who are not fluent in English, often do not measure well in standardized tests. Often it's because of language difficulties. Raub teachers, such as Subervi and Sharon Entrot, help new students navigate the school system, help them learn, and prepare them for the tests. For that, Raub principal Regina M. Finlayson is grateful.

Alex says he gets mostly Cs and Bs. He needs more time to improve, he says.

"I have only been here a year," he says. "I can't speak English. I'm still new."

Alex at times knows the answers to Missus's questions, but doesn't know how to respond in English.

On this day, Missus reviews the lesson on the water cycle. Alex understands how the water from rivers flows to the oceans, evaporates to the sky, and comes down as rain, and that the cycle is repeated.

"OK, give me something related to water," Missus says. Alex raises his hand, as if he is trying to reach the ceiling. He knows the answer. Missus calls on him.

Alex opens his mouth to speak and pauses. "Los arboles y el pasto, Missus," he says.

Missus thanks him for the answer, but asks him to try in English. "Do not help him!" she cautions the other students.

"What are arboles in English, Missus?" he asks. He thinks for a few seconds. "Oh, trees and grass, Missus, they need water."

Missus knows that Alex understands the subject and just needs help with the translation. But he's not the only one who needs her attention.

There is Tofeek Alhadad, an Arabic student who prefers not to speak in his native language, in order to fit in, but who struggles with English grammar. There is Iye Kamara from Africa, who was unable to recognize her name on a piece of paper or pick up a pencil at the beginning of the school year. There is also Lumnije Hasani, or "Lume," who fled war-torn Kosovo and is still learning how to write in English. And Toan Tran from Vietnam, the oldest and tallest in the class. He is impatient and has been asking for a year how long it will take to master English.

Whenever Missus is unable to communicate verbally with a student, because of the language barriers, she will use pictures and computer images to make her point. To teach the word "bear," she showed the students a photo of Winnie the Pooh on a book cover, and they nodded to show they understood.

There are many students from Puerto Rico and Latin America who insist on speaking Spanish, or often Spanglish, a combination of Spanish and English, in class.

But Missus tries not to slip into speaking Spanish. The more the students hear and practice English, she says, the faster they will learn it. She understands her students' frustrations. She was an ESOL student in second grade when her family moved to New York from the Dominican Republic.

She begins lectures by repeating her words and sentences.

Some students understand her the first time and get bored with the repetition. Others need to hear it for days before they can process and understand the information, she knows.

In Spanish class, where he is mastering Spanish language rules, Alex feels most comfortable. He can speak Spanish and be rewarded for it. He can spell his name, A-L-E-X-A-N-D-E-R, and pronounce every letter correctly and give help to other students.

Some of his other successes occur outside the classroom, away from the eyes— and ears—of the Missus. In the lunch room, where the majority of the students are English speakers, ESOL students try to fit in by speaking English, or risk being called a dummy, Alex and his friends say.

On this lunch hour, Alex taps the lunch table with his hands in rhythm with a girl from his ESOL class. A taller boy walks by, and the girl takes a glance. Alex notices.

"Hey," Alex shouts out. "She like you."

The boy stops for a few seconds and asks, "Who?"

"She like you," he repeats and points at her.

The boy giggles and walks away. But Alex is proud. He spoke in English, and was understood.

"I'm learning," Alex says. "I am liking it here."

14

GRADING THE PARENTS

Nitza Colon doesn't give up easily, especially when trying to coax Latino parents into attending Parent-Teacher Organization meetings at Marvine Elementary School in Bethlehem.

So on this afternoon, hours before a scheduled meeting, the PTO leader asks her friend and co-worker Linda Lopez if she'll attend.

Lopez, a school secretary, replies that she would like to but cannot leave work early. And after work, she has to be home to care for her seven-year-old foster child and to cook dinner.

Colon thanks her and goes on, mindful of the demands on parents but determined to boost parental involvement at the school.

"They tell me they are tired, have to take care of their younger children, the husband wants the dinner on the table," Colon says. "There are many reasons why they cannot show up."

Attempts to get Latino parents more involved in their children's education are not limited to Marvine. The same happens to the rest of the schools where Latinos make up large chunks of the student population in the Lehigh Valley.

The reason? Latino children, as well as African American children, are more likely than their white counterparts to fail in school, and lack of parental involvement is partly to blame, according to a study by the National Assessment of Educational Performance.

To spur involvement, area schools send out notices in Spanish and English. Administrators hire bilingual staff. Some schools, such as William Allen High School in Allentown, serve Puerto Rican rice and beans and hire disc jockeys to play salsa and Spanish hip-hop, all to create an environment familiar to Latinos.

"Getting [Latino] parents involved is difficult, but you need that if you want the children to succeed," said Abe Karahoca, who heads Allen's English for Speakers of Other Languages (ESOL) department. "Most parents come here when their kids face disciplinary action, not for positive moments. They are predisposed to think they come to school to get bad news."

Latino parents keep a distance for many reasons—language barriers, cultural differences and, if parents and their children are illegal immigrants, a fear of deportation, educators say. Also, modern-day pressures, including jobs, leave little time for parents of all ethnic groups to participate.

"Only a Few Loyal Ones"

At Marvine, where about 80 percent of the students are Latino, Colon is president, secretary, and treasurer of the PTO. She has been president for more than six years and wants someone to take her place. She is not hopeful. Usually between twenty and thirty parents attend the PTO meetings, but only four parents show up today, despite her making dozens of phone calls.

"I have only a few loyal ones," she says.

Colon began by holding meetings at 4 p.m., when she figured it would be easier to coax parents to stay when they come to pick up their children. That hasn't worked, so she'll try holding meetings later, possibly at 6:15 p.m., when parents might be finished with work and dinner.

"These are only once a month," she said. "I am sure parents can find an hour or so a month. Get a babysitter, or something."

At most meetings, parents usually talk about their children's curriculum and how to approach teachers with complaints or questions.

Colon, who works at the school, stops by some of her son's classes, especially math, where he needs help. "I don't want to tell him 'I don't know,' so I often stay after class to ask the teacher questions," she said.

Most Latino parents want the best for their children but are not sure how to make that happen in the American school system. In Puerto Rico and some Latin American countries, parents do not need to make appointments to see a teacher or a principal. In the United States, they have to fill out paperwork and write letters when a child misses school.

And then there is the language barrier, says Patricia Terreros, an ESOL teacher at Allen. Many parents do not speak or write the language they need to approach teachers and principals.

"They are lost," Karahoca says. "I would be, too."

One parent, who is an illegal immigrant, said she doesn't attend parent-teacher meetings in part because she fears officials will find out her status.

"I have to be careful of the steps I take," the woman said. "One wrong move and we can be deported."

Jobs interfere at times, because many first-generation Latino parents work long hours at more than one job.

Overcoming those obstacles is more important than ever to help parents find their way, since Latinos now make up more than 45 percent of the Allentown School District's student body. Latinos make up more than 30 percent of Bethlehem Area's students and 9 percent of Easton Area schools.

Breaking the Ice

In Allentown, some teachers have taken classes to learn about the language and cultural aspects of Puerto Rico.

Other teachers try to meet parents when they pick up their children at school, said Ana Sainz de la Pena, a former Allentown ESOL coordinator.

"We know that some of our new parents need more than a letter," de la Pena said. "We need to break the ice with them."

Some of the Bethlehem Area elementary schools with high concentrations of Latinos employ staff to reach out to parents. They visit parents at home and educate them about how to approach a school official or teacher, said Iris Cintron, district coordinator of minority affairs for Bethlehem schools. Bilingual secretaries can help Spanish speakers navigate the system.

Easton Area school officials also have initiatives such as sending out notices in English and Spanish. And ESOL teachers are encouraged to have close contact with parents, said Tom Kopetskie, the district's director of curriculum instruction.

School officials know that they need more programs to increase long-term participation. They want Latino parents to volunteer at schools, run for school board positions, and propose new ideas.

"We are not where we need to be," Cintron said, "but we are going in the right direction."

15

LATINO MEDICINE

The office does not look much different from an average hospital suite. The walls are ivory white. Television sets show the news. Nurses walk in and out carrying folders. Some people wait patiently for their appointments. Others worry about a loved one inside.

But this is not your typical clinic. The difference starts at the door, literally. The door sign reads: "Centro de Salud LatinoAmericano. . . . Su Cultura. Su Idioma. Su Salud" (Center for Latin American Health. . . . Your Culture. Your Language. Your Health). This is in the middle of Lehigh Valley Hospital, one of the major hospital chains in the area, at Seventeenth and Chew streets in Allentown.

The medical providers here are not just required to speak Spanish. They are also required to understand many different aspects of Latino culture. Luisa Zambrano, in her late seventies, knows this. That's why on this day she does not have to worry about walking in alone. Once she has taken the elevator to the second story and walked past the English-language offices, she settles in the hospital's Latino section and waits her turn to see the doctor.

"It's very special to be in a place where people speak your language," Zambrano says. "I feel so much joy when I'm here."

This Latino corner is the creation of Dr. Edgar Maldonado, a native of Puerto Rico who came to the Lehigh Valley to complete his residency in 2001. He soon landed a permanent position as a general practitioner.

Being one of the few Latino and Spanish-speaking doctors at the hospital, he found himself bombarded with Spanish-speaking patients. With Latinos making up more than a quarter of the city's population, he sensed a need for more than just one busy doctor taking on a large number of Spanish speakers. So in June 2004, he got the hospital's backing to open the region's first all-Spanish-speaking clinic.

He hopes that other area hospitals follow his lead. As it is, Latinos lack adequate medical health care, Maldonado and other Latino activists in the area say.

While this is the only Latino-oriented clinic of its type, many area hospitals have been taking measures to serve a growing Spanish-speaking population, says Myra Denisse Pina, a program coordinator with an organization called Latinos for Healthy Communities located in downtown Allentown.

In mid-2004 Latino activists organized a meeting with eight leading hospitals in north and central Pennsylvania. They all pledged to increase the number of Spanish-speaking translators in their hospitals. The organization offered to train them, if the hospitals would pay the cost.

"The demographics are changing so fast, but unfortunately, the services aren't," Pina, who is also an M.D., says.

The hospitals are in the process of increasing the number of translators at their offices and facilities, sending a handful to be trained at the organization. Latino health leaders plan to schedule follow-up meetings with the hospitals to check on their progress regularly.

Dr. Luis Campos, a private doctor and general surgeon in the area, says he encourages other Spanish-speaking doctors to come to the Lehigh Valley.

"Many people ask me, 'Wouldn't that be competition for you?' and I say no, of course not. We need many, many more," Campos says.

That's why Maldonado's clinic will remain more than popular; it is needed desperately by Spanish-speaking patients in the Lehigh Valley. The staff includes physicians Maldonado and Maria Jones; case manager Cindy Attamian; physician's assistant Betty Bohorquez; registered nurse Adelines Betancourt; and two medical assistants, Sheyla Torres and Stephanie Roque. The clinic sees an average of thirty patients per day.

"We need a bigger space. We don't even advertise. We can't," Maldonado says one day between consultations. "There is a tremendous need for health care like this."

Understanding Latino culture is an important aspect of health care, Maldonado says. Many Latinos often try to cure their illnesses at home with teas and herbs. They see a doctor when all of their home remedies fail. Often, that can be too late. Maldonado, having been raised in Puerto Rico, knows all about these types of short-term treatments. He often takes to the streets to educate Latinos about proper health care in community centers and at health fairs.

He also stresses that he can help Latino patients find financial assistance. "I don't want people to avoid coming because they don't have economic means," he says.

Latinos in the Lehigh Valley, and all over the nation, tend to have high incidences of diabetes, high blood pressure, heart failure, and other dangerous health conditions. Many lack information about HIV.

"Prevention is something new to many Latinos" Maldonado says. "Before we opened here, many people did not have a place to go to."

That includes husband and wife Jose Navarette, in his mid-forties, and Gloria Morales, in her late thirties. Both come here regularly for all of their health care needs. "It's a blessing," Morales says.

But it hasn't always been. When Morales's mother visited other area hospitals, because of the language barrier, she was not able to tell doctors about her symptoms. Then, one day Morales brought her mom to the Lehigh Valley Hospital's emergency room. She met Maldonado. "He was the first to diagnose her with cancer," Morales recalls. "He told her, 'I gotta be honest with you. Your cancer is too advanced, but we will do our best.'"

"She died shortly after," she says, in 2004.

The couple decided from that day on to leave all other medical providers and come to Maldonado for all of their medical needs. Navarette had had his left foot amputated at another hospital, but he decided to see Maldonado for his follow-ups.

"He was not healing," Morales says. "The doctor fixed him. Now he is walking."

Navarette shakes his head in agreement and smiles.

"It's true," he says.

The patients' loyalties often follow Maldonado outside the clinic. He's become something similar to a public figure, but instead of being asked for an autograph, he's asked for medical advice.

"People see me in stores and they start asking me questions. I do store aisle consultations. I don't have a day off," he says jokingly.

The unique ethnic health care system has gotten the attention of many people in the area. Several organizations in the state, including the state's Department of Health, the Pennsylvania Statewide Latino Coalition, the Governor's Advisory Committee on Latino Affairs, and many others have recognized Maldonado's clinic.

On this day, Maldonado says goodbye to Zambrano. She stays behind and thinks for a second. She fiddles with her purse to buy a few minutes. Her facial expression changes from confused to confident. She approaches Sheyla Torres, one of the medical assistants, and tells her in Spanish, "I need to schedule a mammogram." She pauses and goes on: "Oh, and also a flu shot."

In the past, she would have had a difficult time making these simple medical requests. In the past, she would receive only the treatments volunteered to her by her English-speaking doctors. On this day, she walks away with a smile. She no longer has to leave her medical treatment to fate and her poor English. Here, she says, she feels at home.

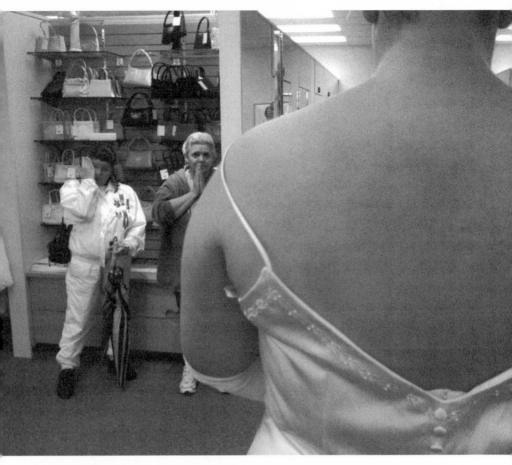

(above) Mom and grandma tear up when Nerivonne Sanchez finds her dress for the quinceañera celebration. Photo: Frank Wiese.

(left) Quinceañera Nerivonne Sanchez is escorted by her uncle Nelson Bermudez. Photo: Frank Wiese.

Nerivonne Sanchez opens presents with friends. Photo: Frank Wiese.

Principal David Vazquez takes a second to ponder the fate of his students. Photo: Frank Wiese.

(right) Worker Abelardo Lopez makes time go faster by singing in the fields. Photo: Arturo Fernandez.

(below) Migrant worker Alfredo Sanchez looks at photos of his wife and daughter. Photo: Arturo Fernandez.

Alfredo Sanchez drives workers to farms in the Shenandoah, Pennsylvania, area. Photo: Arturo Fernandez.

Alfredo Sanchez leads workers to the next field. Photo: Arturo Fernandez.

David DeJesus Jr. stands proud after defending his mom and sister from a home intruder. Photo: Frank Wiese

Elsa Vazquez deals with dual identity every day, being black and Latina. Photo: Frank Wiese.

Juan Orta embraces both his Latino and African heritage by playing the
pango. Photo: Frank Wiese.

(above) Alex Londono raises his hand to answer a question during ESOL class. Photo: Cesar L. Laure.

(left) Alex Londono struggles to learn English as a new arrival from Colombia. Photo: Cesar L. Laure.

(below) ESOL teacher Carmen Subervi, known as "Missus," teaches English as a second language to new arrivals. Photo: Cesar L. Laure.

Andy Bermudez attends tutoring after class to finish his GED and get a better job. Photo: Ed Crisostomo.

Andy Bermudez fills out a job application after dropping out from high school. Photo: Ed Crisostomo.

Youth mentor Carlos Reyes makes sure that Andy finishes his GED homework. Photo: Ed Crisostomo.

(left) Catholic brother
Alfonso Bonilla prays
at church. Photo: Don
Fisher.

(below) Brother Bonilla
prays with prisoners.
Photo: Don Fisher.

Brother Bonilla
reads the Bible.
Photo: Don Fisher.

A member of Deportivo Colorines plays soccer with white players. Photo: Ed Crisostomo.

Aneht Argueta said that she came to the United States to fulfill her dreams of giving her son a better life. Photo: Betty E. Cauler.

Naomi Eda Zelaya before she died in a tragic pedestrian accident.

Alejandro Rodriguez carries a heavy cross during a re-creation of Jesus's crucifixion. Photo: Ed Crisostomo.

Parishioners cry when Alejandro Rodriguez re-creates Jesus's death. Photo: Ed Crisostomo.

Bartolo Figueroa and his friend Genesis Pagano test his new wheelchair around the block. Photo: Arturo Fernandez.

Bartolo Figueroa gambles to pass the time in this small Puerto Rican town. Photo: Arturo Fernandez.

Bartolo Figueroa ponders leaving behind his family in Pennsylvania to return to his hometown in Patillas, Puerto Rico. Photo: Arturo Fernandez.

HOOKED ON TELENOVELAS

When the clock hits 7 p.m., Evelyn Lopez knows where to find her daughter Wanda Diaz. She is glued to the television set, watching Spanish-language soap operas.

Diaz's favorite telenovela is *Carita de Angel* (Angel Face), which follows the antics of a seven-year-old girl who often gets into trouble in a private Catholic school run by nuns.

On this weeknight, Lopez, Diaz, and other family members gather around the television to watch the latest episode. Everyone giggles when the young character opens a box inside the principal's office and a frog jumps out. The principal, an elderly nun, passes out.

"She can make us laugh and cry," Lopez says of the young character. "She is soooo smart for her age. She always knows what to do. She is so smooth."

"Oh, mom," says Diaz. "I always cry when I see her suffer."

Lopez and Diaz are among the millions of Latino viewers who are choosing prime-time Spanish-language telenovelas over English-language shows, including highly rated shows on English channels, such as *Friends* and *ER*.

More than half of Latino homes prefer Spanish-language programming to English-language programming, according to Nielsen ratings.

More like a miniseries, a telenovela will air every night from Monday through Friday, and sometimes on weekends, with an average run of six months to a year. Main characters go through several transformations.

Many Latinos watch these shows to stay in touch with their cultural roots. And Spanish-language networks, such as Univision and Telemundo, know that they can attract Latinos' attention by airing programs they used to see in their native countries. Many Latino parents don't want their children to lose their native language and culture. The telenovelas help to reinforce traditions.

Gladys Lugo, who lives in downtown Allentown, says that as soon as she watches the first episode of a telenovela, she is sold, and she watches it until it ends. She is a fan of *Carita de Angel* as well as *Amigas y Rivales* (Girlfriends and Rivals) and *Por un Beso* (For a Kiss).

Most afternoons, she takes a break from a long day and watches her favorite stories with her two elementary-school-aged children, Jose and Coral.

"Sometimes when I want to go to the bathroom, I hold it until the commercials come up," Lugo says. "I cannot go anywhere when they are on."

Lugo says she also learns new words by watching the telenovelas and enjoys seeing the scenery of countries such as Mexico, Venezuela, and Argentina, where most telenovelas aired in the United States are produced.

"I have never been to those countries, but you kind of go there by watching the novelas," she says.

Univision, the largest and most popular Spanish-language channel in the United States, saw its ratings for telenovelas increase 30 percent over the past years, including among teenage and male viewers. *Carita de Angel*, when it aired in 2001, was the most-watched program in the Los Angeles market among all eighteen- to fifty-four-year-olds, also beating television shows such as *Friends*, *The Simpsons*, *The Drew Carey Show*, and *Seinfeld*, according to Univision and the national rating data.

To keep up with the demand, the rival Spanish-language network Telemundo has recently beefed up its prime-time lineup. And in the next few years, some television insiders have said, all television networks will likely add more Latino characters to their prime-time lineups to attract more Latino viewers.

But for now, networks Univision and Telemundo and the cable television channel Galavision know that the fastest way to reach Latinos is by giving them what they want—telenovelas.

For Venerosa De Jesus, who left Puerto Rico as a child and now lives in Allentown, the Spanish-language soaps provide a strong link to her native land. She has seldom gone back to the island, but still remembers its warm climate and friendly people. She gets to relive those days when she watches telenovelas that take place in the countryside.

Most of the shows she watches are exports from Mexico, Venezuela, and other Latin American countries. De Jesus loves the story lines. She has tried watching English-language soaps, but she finds that the story lines drag on too long and the plots develop slowly. Spanish-language telenovelas move along faster, she says.

"This is why I like them," she says. "You are glued to your TV screen."

In a typical story line, a young woman from a small town arrives in a big city. She falls in love with a rich and handsome young man. She overcomes evil rivals, ends up in prison, gets pregnant, and loses her baby. Later in the story, the main character regains her freedom, her baby, and the love of her life.

"I like stories about love," De Jesus says. "We are so busy with our lives that at the end of the day, you want to sit down and watch a good story."

Some newer telenovelas, including a few produced in the United States, are incorporating social issues into their story lines, but it's not happening fast enough, says Meyling Eliash, national director of communications for the Mexican American Legal Defense and Educational Fund.

"The Spanish-language channels air telenovelas almost all day long," Eliash says. "Spanish-speaking viewers really do not have much choice. The least they could do is use telenovelas as a vehicle to educate Latinos."

Some shows, however, have included the issues of substance abuse, sexually transmitted diseases, and sexuality in their story lines. On the telenovela *La Vida en el Espejo* (Seeing Your Life in the Mirror), which aired on Telemundo in 2001, character Mauricio Roman deals with problems that could affect any family. His parents split up. His mother is having an affair with her young assistant. His brother is getting help to overcome substance abuse. His girlfriend is mad at him because he will not engage in premarital sex. And he finds himself staring at the muscular, Speedo-clad men walking by a pool, questioning his sexuality.

Some rural areas in Latin America and in third world countries used to air radio novelas in the 1960s. They used the airwaves not only to entertain people but also to inform them about social issues and current events in their countries.

"We need more of that," Eliash echoes.

On this weeknight, Diaz watches *Carita de Angel* with her mother and two cousins in her small living room. Diaz says she watches telenovelas about five nights a week, and about three hours each night.

Her cousins Tiffany and Timothy Wiederhold like to watch *Amigas y Rivales*, a story about five girls who will test their friendship over young guys. "That one has more young people in it," Tiffany says.

Since telenovelas are mainly filmed in Mexico and other Latin American countries, Diaz sometimes has trouble understanding the informal Spanish expressions. In a recent episode of *Carita de Angel*, a little girl tricks a nun into taking her to see a friend in a poor part of Mexico. The nun catches onto the girl's lie and confronts her: "No te hagas la turista. Para que me dijiste que te trajera"—literally, "Don't act like a tourist. Why did you want me to bring you here?" But what the nun means is, "Don't act like you don't know what I am talking about. Why did you want me to bring you here?" Diaz has learned to pick up on the slang, and she says she enjoys the overall plots.

Carita de Angel ends and Diaz runs for a snack—a peanut butter sandwich and glass of milk. It is getting dark and her mother must get home. They hug and say their goodbyes. Diaz goes back to her chair. The first soap of the night is over, but the night is not.

She does not plan to miss *Amigas y Rivales*, and the promos for *Por un Beso* look interesting, she says. As long as there are telenovelas on, Diaz plans to watch them all.

A STEP BEHIND

Oscar Cruz never really gave it much thought. He attended Head Start. So what, it was no big deal, says Cruz, now in his twenties.

Yet he remembers what the classroom and the building looked like near his South Bethlehem home, and he keeps pictures of his fifth birthday party organized by his Head Start teachers and friends. Officially, the government calls it a federally funded comprehensive preschool program for children from low-income families. But Cruz's mother, Petra, calls it a life changer.

Of her three children, Oscar was the one she could not control. At four years old, he was angry most of the time. But he slowly changed into a calmer, more humble child after attending Head Start, says his mother.

Cruz is not unique. Head Start has helped turn hundreds of reclusive or angry children into successful students, especially here, where Latino children tend to fall further behind than other struggling students.

The road from passive or aggressive to outgoing and successful is not always easy. But that does not keep Head Start employees from trying. Teachers and administrators spend many hours getting to know a child and his or her parents to try to get to the root of the child's problems.

Sometimes parents—who may work more than one job and need help around the house—give their children too many chores, leaving little time for homework. Other times a child may be witnessing violence at home or suffering from other distractions. Head Start workers try to identify these problems early and refocus the child's attention on school, learning, and games, said Lorraine Weidman, with Head Start of the Lehigh Valley.

"We target low-income children because they are the ones at a disadvantage," Weidman said.

Low-income parents spend much of their time working, trying to make enough money to buy tomorrow's groceries or pay next month's rent. Middle- and upper-class children usually get more attention from their parents and have books and learning games that help them feel more at ease around peers and in the classroom.

The federal government created Head Start in 1965 to help children with poor social skills succeed in public education settings. More than 30,000 children participate in the Head Start program statewide, according to the Pennsylvania Head Start Association. The number of Head Start families in the Lehigh Valley has grown steadily in the past few years to about a thousand children in the early 2000s, with about three hundred more on a waiting list. About 10 percent of new students suffer from some kind of disability.

Eighty percent of the program's $5 million budget comes from the federal government, with the rest from local sources. A family of four must make less than $17,000 a year and show a need for the program to qualify.

"And believe me, we have larger families who make less than that," said Weidman. "We wish we could help every child, but we can't."

More than half of the Head Start children are Latinos who are barely learning their native Spanish language while trying to master English. And that makes their transition much more difficult.

Local Head Start officials said their hard work has paid off. In the summer of 2000, the New York–based National Association for the Education of Young Children accredited the last of the twenty-one classrooms operated by the local Head Start throughout the Lehigh Valley. The organization has some of the strictest classroom standards in the country.

Those strict but caring rules helped turn Cruz into the responsible adult he now is, his mother said.

"But you should have seen him as a child," she said. "Oscar was an angry child. So angry that he would jump, cry, scream, and tear the houseplants apart to get his point across."

"One day I spanked him because he only left the stem on a plant," Petra recalled, holding back giggles.

Cruz flips through the pages of his photo album. The first photo shows him wearing a king's crown. He laughs at the picture of him blowing out birthday candles. He views more photos and tries to remember more about his childhood. Some images are blurry, but he remembers why he became so angry at times, he says. He was not a bad child.

"The cage," he says out loud.

"Oh, right," his mom repeats. "That cage."

His days of anger go back to one of his first hospital visits. He was about one year old when his mother noticed he had trouble breathing. She took him to a hospital, but he became angry and frustrated with every labored breath. The doctors and nurses could not control him, so they locked him in a cage-like crib to keep him from falling down.

Petra Cruz said the source of his breathing problem was a severe sinus infection and that doctors eventually helped him breathe normally, but he said he was not the same after that day. He had constant nightmares of being inside a cage, looking out and wondering if he would ever get out.

He was a "lonely child," without siblings to talk to or play with, his mom said, until one day when she heard somebody talking about a program called Head Start.

She took him by the hand into a room full of children like him, with a pleasant, tall woman whose smile complemented every other word.

Cruz did not feel lonely anymore. He began making friends and he became interested in books.

Head Start officials usually set up classrooms to inspire this kind of reaction in new students, many of whom have not been exposed to books, games, and caring teachers.

For many, this is their first time away from mom. Some children are very aggressive. They cannot talk, so the only way they can express their emotions is through violent, angry acts.

To make the children feel more at ease, the teachers try to make the classroom a fun place and divide it into four sections. The first is a role-play area, where children can dress up, try out different clothes, and pretend to be the mom or dad.

The second is a construction area, where children can learn to build their own little houses or bridges with blocks. Teachers describe them as little architects.

In a section called "the sensorial area," children can touch and smell items. They can squeeze an orange and drink the juice, for example. The learning section is where children can pick up books and read and repeat new words that they are learning.

Teachers meet with parents, and together they create an individual plan for each of the twenty children per classroom in Allentown, Bethlehem, and Easton.

They don't expect the children to be reading and writing at this level. They simply hope to increase the children's interest in books so they can learn to discover a new world once they go on to first grade.

Once Cruz went to first grade, he felt comfortable talking to other children and reading words one by one.

However, classroom instruction is often not enough. Head Start teachers and administrators strive to teach adults how to become better parents. Parents learn the basics about nutrition, communication skills, and tips on how they can show interest in their children's education.

The distractions in a poor home, besides keeping children from learning, sometimes even keep them from getting the medical care they need, said Nancy Martin, Head Start's director of family partnerships.

Most of the children do not have medical insurance. Head Start tries to make sure that children are getting health and dental care.

Kaye Silberman, now in her fifties, benefited from the parenting skills she learned about twenty years ago when she enrolled her daughter in Head Start. She used to question her skills as a mother and had low self-esteem.

Martin said that's not unusual for poor parents who see more affluent families succeeding.

Silberman was on her own with three-year-old Beth when she changed their destiny. "I did not know you could give a child choices instead of just saying no," said Silberman, an office manager at Chiquita Banana in Bethlehem. "She [Beth] was a withdrawn child and became much more verbal and shared more at home after [Head Start]."

Silberman learned to communicate better with her daughter, who now lives in Allentown, to become not only her role model and confidante but also her friend, Silberman said. What mother and daughter learned in Head Start will remain in the family for generations, she added.

"I used to sing 'Wheels on the bus, go round, round, round,' and now I can hear her singing that same song to her child," Silberman said. "It's too bad not all children have access to Head Start."

Head Start created a sister program called Early Head Start in 1995 to give mothers-to-be and new mothers the skills they need to be responsible parents. Social workers visit about seventy-five homes in Allentown and teach child care, such as where to go for medical and nutritional help.

"It's never too early to begin educating a child," said Weidman. "Sometimes it can be too late when we begin helping them when they are five years old."

Cruz says he was glad he was saved from his own anger when he was five. He puts his photo album away and takes a deep breath. He is not sure how his life would have turned out had his mother not dropped him off at Head Start fifteen years ago.

But he sees a bright future. He uses the skills he learned in Head Start on a daily basis. He can communicate with peers, he has a passion for books—especially ones about music—and he plans to graduate from Moravian College in two years with a music-related degree, and then open his own recording company.

"I came out a different person," he said.

His mother smiles in agreement.

18

CITY BOYS

Andy Bermudez dropped out of William Allen High School, the biggest and most racially diverse high school in the Lehigh Valley.

He felt lost in the classroom.

He was a freshman. A seventeen-year-old freshman. A six-foot-two, 183-pound freshman with an F average.

Too old, too big, too dumb. That's how he felt.

He can almost hear the giggles of his former younger classmates. Sure, they laughed at him, but they didn't bother to find out why he lagged behind.

They did not know that his father drank himself to death when he was twelve, that his role models were two older brothers who constantly got in trouble with police, that he felt ignored by his teachers. "I never had a role model, a person who went to high school in my family," he said.

Now, without a high school education, Bermudez feels lost in the real world.

At his mother's insistence, he began working toward a general equivalency diploma, or GED. He attends classes at the Hispanic American Organization in downtown Allentown. He signed up within weeks of dropping out of Allen High School and went looking for a job.

Bermudez will need to pass all the GED tests in subjects such as English, math, and science before he can get his certificate. He has yet to take his first test, but plans to as soon as he feels ready.

In GED class on a recent weeknight, he scribbles some numbers on his notepad.

$28 \times .06 =$

The numbers and equations were a language he did not understand in high school. He shakes his head. Now he knows this, he thinks.

Teacher Amanda Sechrist explains, step by step, how to solve the equation. Bermudez's eyes follow her right hand at the chalkboard. Zero times 8 and 2, and 6 times 8 and 2.

$28 \times .06 = 168$

"Where does the period go?" Sechrist asks.

Bermudez wants to whisper that the period goes before the 6. But he hesitates. What if he is wrong? He'll wait for the teacher to give the answer. The others do too.

"Before the 6. The answer is 1.68."

Right, he murmurs.

He jots down 1.68.

He feels smart.

Finally.

When he was fifteen, Bermudez's mother sent him to the Netherlands to live with an older brother who had moved there with a family friend and turned his life around. The move helped Bermudez too, but he came back to Allentown when his mother fell ill. He started up where he had left off, as a high school freshman. But at age seventeen.

At the GED classes, things are different from high school. He is the youngest in class. His teacher knows his name. His name, Andy Bermudez.

She calls on him now and then. He acts as if he does not want to be bothered. He pauses, looks at the ceiling before slowly responding. He likes the attention, and that a teacher believes he knows an answer.

The class ends, and it is time to go home or maybe hang out with buddies from Eighth Street, many of whom also dropped out of school and are trying to figure out what to do with their lives.

The following Monday, Bermudez wakes to find Carlos Reyes, a youth mentor, knocking on his door on South Eighth Street, where he lives with his mother and a brother. It's 10 a.m. Time to find a job.

Reyes is the closest thing Bermudez has to a male role model. He provides encouragement and is trying to help him get a job and ahead in life.

Bermudez gets dressed—baggy jeans, loose T-shirt, heavy chains around his neck, and a thick silver medallion with the words "Puerto Rico" standing out. He knows Reyes asked him to dress "more appropriately," but he woke up late and it is time to go.

Both get in Reyes's blue 1996 Saturn and head to the Lehigh Valley Mall. On their way, Bermudez tells Reyes that he does not want to work in fast food or a "dirty job" like cleaning.

Reyes nods, but he warns him that it is not going to be easy. After all, he does not have a high school diploma.

But Bermudez is optimistic. He can stock store shelves. That would be cool, he says.

They drive and Reyes glances at Bermudez, who is staring at passing cars, silent. Reyes knows Bermudez is bright and could do much more than stock merchandise at a store. He has seen the same profile in many other "city boys," as he calls them—teens who have never met their fathers or who have bad relationships with them, who became confused or angry. Some blame their mothers because their fathers left. If Bermudez had had a father figure growing up, maybe he would still be in high school, getting decent grades.

They stop at several mall stores. Bermudez fills out application after application. The managers look at his application. No high school diploma. GED not completed.

"We'll call you if there is an opening," most say.

And Bermudez walks away.

He tells Reyes he is planning to move out on his own. Maybe with his girlfriend.

Reyes nods. "You need a job, an income," he says softly, trying to get him to realize what it'll take to survive on his own. But he knows Bermudez will have to learn life's lessons the hard way.

"Just keep looking [for a job]," Reyes tells him. "Living on your own is not as easy as you might think."

After weeks of looking for work, Bermudez lands a full-time job at a fast-food restaurant in Whitehall Township.

It is not the "clean" job he wanted, and he is beginning to realize that life does not necessarily work out as planned. At least now he will be able to pay his own rent, he says.

"I changed my mind," he says, explaining his decision to work at a restaurant. "It's too hard to find any other job."

19

SPANGLISH

Listen to hairstylist Deyaniris Taveras as she cuts hair at Lissy's Beauty Salon at Fourth and Tilghman streets in Allentown.

"Look, su pelo va a quedar como light brown," Taveras tells her boss Lissy Mendez. (Look, her hair will look light brown.)

"Ella se esta viendo su look," Taveras says, as her client examines her hair color in the mirror. (She is checking out her new look.)

She gives her client advice: "Ya esta ready." (It is ready.)

"Don't use spray or jelly on your hair. Te queda todo duro. Nada mas usa un conditioner." (It will make it stiff. Just use a conditioner.)

Call it Spanglish—mixing Spanish and English words in the same sentence and conversation, or applying Spanish grammar rules and pronunciations to English words to create a new vocabulary. For example, "ar" is a common word ending in Spanish, so "to click" becomes *clikear* (clik-eh-ahr) in Spanglish.

Spanglish is spoken by those who speak both English and Spanish so frequently that they begin to use the languages interchangeably, sometimes without being aware they are doing it.

Its popularity extends beyond the Latino neighborhoods of the Lehigh Valley. Spanglish can be heard on Spanish radio and television ads, on stations like Univision and Telemundo, and it is spreading on the Internet, said Deborah Charnes Vallejo, a representative of the Texas advertising firm Bromley Communications.

"It's cool, it's funky, to switch from one language to another," Vallejo said. "It is also very realistic. Latinos speak Spanglish almost everywhere."

The melding of languages is not new. Many modern-day languages evolved from a combination of other languages, according to Scott Baird, a linguistics professor at Trinity University in San Antonio.

Baird says that the melding of languages dates as far back as the origin of language itself. English evolved from a mixture of Danish, German, and Celtic languages. In the early 1060s, when the English and the French shared land and cultures, the English language was heavily influenced by French. It took hundreds of years for people not to notice that they were combining languages, he said, "and it became one."

Today Spanglish is especially popular among Latinos in their teens and twenties. Young Latinos live in an English world during the day, at schools and jobs. But when they go home to their parents and relatives, they sometimes have to communicate in Spanish, and switching between the two often results in Spanglish.

"Spanglish is very popular among high school students," said Eli Vazquez, a counselor at Liberty High School in Bethlehem. "I hear it in the halls, in the classrooms. It's just the way many young people communicate nowadays."

Taveras attends masseuse classes, where she is the only Spanish speaker, and she deals with English-speaking vendors at the salon. But she uses Spanish and Spanglish with clients, friends, and family.

She simply combines words that she knows well in Spanish and English by instinct, she says. Spanglish has become so common for her that her customers always understand her.

Spanglish will become more popular as the community grows, says Erika Sutherland, a Spanish professor at Muhlenberg College and founder of Grupo Apoyo, a support organization for immigrants with college degrees in Allentown.

Latinos make up about a quarter of Allentown's population and their numbers are growing in the rest of the Lehigh Valley.

Many of Sutherland's students ask her about words they have heard on the streets, such as *lonchera* (loan-chay-rah), and want to know if they are new Spanish words. Lonchera is the Spanglish word for lunch box. There is no direct translation in Spanish, other than defining it as a box in which lunch is placed. "The students hear this and they do not know if they have missed something," Sutherland said. "Is it bad Spanish? No, I tell them. But it is not Spanish either. If they are writing an essay, I expect them to use only Spanish. But I tell them they can use Spanglish in an informal setting, because that is how people speak."

Some of Bromley Communication's most popular television commercials feature Spanglish to attract a young Latino population. In a commercial for Charmin toilet paper, a plumber talking to his client, says, "Es que la tuberia esta muy vieja. Esta broke (*brok-ay*)." (The piping is too old. It is broken.)

"Most viewers did not really stop to think, 'Hey, that guy is speaking in English on a Spanish station,'" Vallejo said. The point of the commercial was to make it seem so casual that people identify with the tone of the conversation, she said.

Teenagers Angel Nieves and Carlos Colon spoke Spanglish over pizza at Villarosa's in center-city Allentown. They were passing time with youth mentor Carlos Reyes before playing basketball at a nearby park.

"I got out of school and la vi a ella, le di un besito," says Nieves, a seventhgrader. (I saw her. I gave her a little kiss.) "Pero ella se tenia que ir, so I let her go." (But she had to go, so I let her go.)

"Oh," Reyes says. "Va a la misma escuela que tu?" (Does she go to your school?)

"She goes to Raub [Middle School]," says Nieves.

"A lo mejor Carlos la conoce," Reyes says. (Maybe Carlos knows her.)

"Cual es el nombre the ella?" inquires Colon, a fifth-grader. (What is her name?)

"Jazmin."

The teenagers cannot tell the difference between the languages they use. What matters, they say, is that they understand each other.

Colon speaks mostly English at school, but at home he speaks Spanish to his mother and siblings. "My mom says, 'You are Puerto Rican, not American, you have to speak Spanish,' so, that's what I do," Colon says, trying to hold back giggles. "So, I have to speak Spanish."

"O tu mama te da una bofetada," Nieves interrupts, jokingly. (Or your mom will slap you.)

Reyes tells the teenagers it's good to know both English and Spanish. He says it will make them more marketable when they look for jobs. "But you have to speak one or the other," Reyes tells them. "Spanglish is not a language."

Spanglish may have originated in the Southwest, where the largest concentrations of Latinos reside in the United States, linguists say.

Spanish was being spoken there before English settlers arrived in the 1800s, mainly in California, Arizona, New Mexico, and Texas. English became the language of the mainstream, but Spanish was never lost.

Anna Romero, a journalism professor at the Missouri School of Journalism, knows of many families that have combined Spanish and English for generations in her native Santa Fe, New Mexico. "Any word you can possibly switch into Spanish, you will hear it there," Romero said.

She has brought part of her culture to Missouri, where she teaches a class on how to cover minorities in the news media. Her (mostly white) students are intrigued by the influence of the Spanish language on English words.

She explains to students that many Latinos adopt English words and make them sound like Spanish, sometimes by putting Spanish endings on words or applying Spanish sounds to words. For example, "to park" becomes *parkear* (par-kay-ahr), and "I am going to park the car" becomes "Voy a parkear el carro." "Cake" becomes *queque* (kay-kay) and "block" becomes *bloque* (bloh-kay). There are many other examples, she said.

Spanglish could evolve into the dominant language of the United States, Baird said. Phrases such as "hasta la vista, baby" could become part of everyday vocabulary. "It is not going to happen tomorrow or even one hundred years from now," he said. "It will take time, but Spanglish could become our language."

20

THE WORLD TRADE CONNECTION

Carlos Hamilton stared at the sidewalk, just outside his Bronx apartment. His eyes seemed lost, almost half closed. He whispered that night that he had a message for his brother in Allentown: "I'm OK."

Hamilton barely escaped the World Trade Center's North Tower, the first attacked by terrorists on September 11, 2001. For a week, he was not able to talk to his brother, Pedro Hamilton, who lives in Allentown. It was not the distance, he admitted, but a result of his efforts to forget that day.

Pedro eventually learned through relatives that his brother Carlos was alive and well. But as for many people in Allentown, his connection to New York's 9/11 attacks will always remain. Pedro, after all, is one of many New York City residents who left the city in search of a small-town life. He moved to Allentown, but he never lost his connection to the city.

Pedro's confusion began the morning that he saw the shocking images on television of an airplane crashing into the World Trade Center.

"Looking at those images and knowing that my brother was there, I thought the worst had happened," Pedro said. "It is a miracle he is alive."

Just a few minutes before 9 a.m., Carlos Hamilton and a few fellow construction workers were pasting tape on the walls in an office on the eighty-fifth floor. His friend, Victor Guerrero, also from the Bronx, heard a loud noise and both felt the building shake.

Hamilton looked outside and saw smoke and fires from outside the window.

"They must be celebrating something," Hamilton told his friend, who worked for Harris Beach LLP, based in New York City, at the time.

Soon, they saw crowds rushing downstairs. People started screaming that there was an explosion in the building, Hamilton said.

He rushed out, and his friend followed.

"I only looked back once and I saw fire and people panicking," Hamilton said. "It was a nightmare."

He said security officers told some of the workers that there was probably a bomb in the lower levels and asked some of the people to stay put. Many people could not do anything but cry. Others were paralyzed with fear.

Hamilton and Guerrero decided to keep going. As Hamilton rushed down the stairs, he saw legions of firefighters on their way up.

Many of them probably never came out.

Minutes later, Hamilton and his friend were outside the building, he said, but their co-workers stayed behind.

He said he wanted to go back and get them, but felt he could not.

"It is the worst feeling, not to be able to help other people," Hamilton said.

Hamilton and Guerrero saw the building crumble and kept on running. A few hours later, they made it home to the Bronx, where relatives hugged them and cried.

Their decision to leave when they did was a matter of instinct, he said, a second that dictated whether they were to be dead or alive.

A few days after the tragic incident, both men reflected on their luck.

"I don't think I will be able to ever recover from this," Hamilton said. "The images will haunt me for the rest of my life."

"We were not harmed physically," Guerrero said. "But we will never be the same."

Both men returned to work at another site the following week.

"The sooner we go back to normal, the better," Hamilton said.

In Allentown, Pedro Hamilton went home after work to watch the latest news on television. Watching family members searching desperately for their loved ones reminded him how fortunate he and his brother are.

"I could have lost him," Pedro said. "He may not have died, but I think everyone is mourning the losses."

21

LATINOS AGAIN

When Earl Stephen Zeiner was a child and living in Puerto Rico, every January 5, he would leave a shoebox filled with grass and water by his bedside. According to tradition, three kings would come to his home in the middle of the night and leave him presents. He believed the camels would eat the grass and drink the water.

Zeiner would go to bed a little nervous. What if he left the box too close to his ear and the camels chewed it?

Soon, that annual observance of Los Tres Reyes Magos, or three magical kings (wise men), on the night of the Epiphany would end. Zeiner moved to the United States when he was thirteen, and the three kings were replaced by Santa Claus. As the years went by, Zeiner, now in his twenties, immersed himself in American culture.

"I became so Americanized that I forgot where I came from," he said. "My peers did not celebrate the same holidays. It was not part of my environment anymore."

A few years ago, Zeiner, who lives in Hanover Township in Northampton County, decided to revive the Three Kings holiday and other Puerto Rican traditions with his family.

Like Zeiner, a growing number of Latinos in the Lehigh Valley and the rest of the nation are rediscovering their roots. *Hispanic Magazine* once dubbed them "born-again Latinos"—Latinos raised in an English-speaking environment, who speak little Spanish, and who have reached back to embrace their heritage.

The boom in the Latino population and the media focus on Latino pop stars have helped many Americanized Latinos realize that displaying their heritage is trendy, said Frances Aparicio, a Latino studies professor at the University of Illinois in Chicago. Celebrities who display Latino pride, such as Jennifer Lopez and Ricky Martin, have inspired them.

"When they were in high school, they could not take any classes that taught Latino history," she said. "When Latinos get to college, they have an opportunity to learn about their past."

Many become so excited that they begin joining Latino-oriented organizations. "They have this thirst for their Latino heritage," she said.

In the Lehigh Valley and in small towns elsewhere in the United States, Latinos have become more visible in the past decade. In Allentown, they now make up more than a quarter of the population. Those numbers are not far behind in Beth-lehem and Easton, the three biggest cities in the Lehigh Valley.

As their numbers grow, Latinos find it easier to display their heritage in public.

Earlier Irish and German immigrants went through similar tugs-of-war, edu-cators said.

"I think that as Latinos grow older, out of high school, they do not feel the need to fit in with the other kids and become more proud of who they are," said Rafael Collazo, an activist with the U.S. Hispanic Leadership Institute in Philadelphia. "Our language, family and traditions become more important."

Those exploring their roots will collect Latino artifacts, make trips to their homeland, and learn Spanish for the first time, educators said.

Anna Adams, professor of Latino studies at Muhlenberg College, said that a few second- and third-generation Latinos in search of their identity have taken her Latinos in the United States course. Because Latinos make up a small percentage of the total student body, she sees only a few Latinos in her classes. "One time, one student burst into tears when he started learning about Puerto Rico," she said. "He was surprised how much he did not know about his culture."

Gregory Ramos, in his mid-twenties, took Adams's class. He remembered how he felt like an outsider whenever his father, Latino activist Luis Ramos, would take him to see his grandparents on the South Side of Bethlehem, a Latino enclave. His relatives spoke Spanish, a language he did not understand or speak.

At Muhlenberg, he took Spanish courses and is planning to spend a year in Puerto Rico to immerse himself in his culture and language. His dream is to walk into his grandparents' house and speak to them in their native language, to recon-nect with them, he said.

"Growing up, I always considered myself white. I was always with the white crowd. My mother is white, and that was the side I connected with. Now I want to rediscover my Puerto Rican side," said Ramos, who wants to strike a balance between his American side and Latino roots.

For Zeiner, it was easy to blend in with American society. When his parents moved to Pottstown from Puerto Rico, he attended school with mostly white stu-dents. He was tall and had a fair complexion, thanks to his Hungarian and German ancestry on his father's side. Plus he had a German last name. Unless he volun-teered the information, many of his peers did not know that he was born in Puerto Rico. "I looked like them and celebrated holidays the way they did," Zeiner said.

High school and college followed, then law school. Zeiner decided he needed to relive his childhood days.

So he got to work. He compiled a list of Puerto Rican holidays, beginning with Three Kings Day, which revived fond childhood memories. As the tradition goes, Kings Melchor, Gaspar, and Baltasar, in search of the baby Jesus, followed a star and found the infant on January 6.

Zeiner created a Web page to share what he learned with other Americanized Latinos.

Tony Marrero, former president of the Puerto Rican Parade Committee, organizes a Three Kings festivity early in January at Sacred Heart Church in downtown Allentown. Most years, the committee prepares a sketch—in Spanish as well as English, because many youngsters don't speak Spanish anymore—to show the children the difference between Santa Claus and the Three Kings.

"We want children to remember their Latino traditions," Marrero said.

Now that Zeiner feels Latino again, he faces another obstacle: convincing others that he is Latino.

Sometimes he orders in Spanish at Latino restaurants. Employees see a tall, white young man and figure that he is a college student trying to practice his learned Spanish. "I have to mention specific places I know and important figures so they can believe me," he said. "People have their own ideas of what a Puerto Rican person must look like."

Zeiner said his ethnicity is not dictated by the color of his skin, but by cultural pride.

"People may not believe I am a Latino," he said. "But I know I am."

ONE MAN, ONE MISSION

Catholic brother Alfonso Bonilla bends over the sick man lying in bed at his home, holds his right hand, and whispers, "I am praying for you."

He repeats the sentence a few times to make sure the man, who has AIDS, has heard him.

The man's breathing is labored. The bones in his face and arms are noticeable. The man opens his mouth, trying to say something, then shuts it.

"I can see God in you," Alfonso tells him.

Some days are more draining than others, Alfonso knows. After all, he is one of three religious brothers at the Mission Queen of Angels, Convento Misra, in Allentown. The mission is affiliated with the city's Sacred Heart and Our Lady of Mount Carmel churches.

Alfonso, in his early twenties, knows that he could be living close to his family in Costa Rica. He could be dating girls his age, or could be finishing up study for a lucrative career. But he does not think about those possibilities anymore.

Instead, he finds reward in visiting the sick, people who live alone, and those in prison. His life will be even more rewarding, he says, if he becomes a priest.

Some people ask him how he feels about being among the small number of Latinos who are exchanging modern-day commodities for a life of service and humility. Modern-day commodities, though, are something that have been in his way, like wearing a heavy jacket on a hot summer day. No, this is what he wants, being here, holding the hand of a man whom many ignore out of fear.

"If you had asked me a few years ago if I ever thought of becoming a priest, I would have said, What? A priest? You have to be stronger every day."

How can he not want to be a priest here, in a town that has seen more Latinos moving here than most places in America? One out of four residents is Latino. That's what they told him at the church the moment he came: You're needed here, Alfonso. Most people don't speak English. They need guidance. They need you.

Before coming here, he had known that more and more American Catholic bishops were traveling to Puerto Rico and other Latin America countries to identify talented young men who wanted to be priests. These other young men have faced the same pressures from society and their families to pursue fields other than a religious life, just as he has. And yet they have gone to other middle American towns to serve the new residents. And so will he, he tells himself.

Just One Day

Alfonso Bonilla was a typical sixteen-year-old in his native Costa Rica. He liked brand-name clothes and fast music. His parents thought it would be a good idea if he volunteered some of his free time at a senior center in his country.

"At first I did not like it," he remembers. "We had to clean the old people, take care of them. I could not eat for a few days. The first day I went, I told myself I was not going to come back."

But something inside him, a soft voice ringing inside his ears, told him to go back, at least one more day. He did.

Soon he befriended the Catholic brothers training him at the center. He began to admire their lives, which were peaceful and filled with few material possessions. He wanted that internal peace.

Brand-name clothes and parties no longer satisfied him. He wanted more. Maybe, he though, he could find their spirit and help himself find the inner peace he longed for.

By age seventeen he decided to become a brother (and if all works out, a priest) and to dedicate his life to the Catholic Church.

His parents were shocked. They were happy that he wanted to give back to his community. But, they asked, why sacrifice your life? Why give up a future with a wife and children, a job, and Sunday dinners with relatives? Why leave us all and give your life to strangers? Giving up a lifetime of options seemed like a big price to pay, family members told him.

But Alfonso was steadfast.

"I have had many chances to change my mind and I have not done that," he says. "It will not happen."

He had time to test his faith. The first year he lived a dual life, spending half his time with his family and friends and the other half working with the religious brothers.

Over the next two years, he gave up his materialistic life little by little. Finally he vowed to live a life of poverty, chastity, and obedience. All in all, he needs seven years of theological study, living by the same vows, to become a Roman Catholic priest.

In Allentown, he lives with two other young Catholic brothers at the Mission Queen of Angels. Brother Isaac Ledezma, also of Costa Rica, and mentor brother Esteban Berger of Guatemala have become his family here. They share a three-bedroom house on Chew Street in Allentown. They argue, pray, and cook together, Alfonso says, like blood brothers do.

He speaks mostly Spanish, ministering to the Latino community, but he is learning English to reach more people.

A Bible and a Cross

On this day, after waking up at about 6 a.m., the three religious brothers in Allentown say their prayers together at a small chapel in Our Lady of Mount Carmel Church on Chew Street. After breakfast, they say their goodbyes and each take off at about 8 a.m. to visit people in the community who are sick or need company.

Alfonso wears a dark gray robe and wooden cross around his neck and carries a Bible that fits in the palm of his hand. I have what I need, he says to himself.

One of his first stops is a center-city house, about a fifteen-minute walk from his home. He sees an older woman sitting on her porch, holding an open Bible and looking at the sky.

He calls out "abue," short for grandmother in Spanish. The woman is no more than five feet tall. Felicita Hernandez, in her eighties, looks over and sees him.

She can no longer walk to Sacred Heart Church, so Alfonso brings Communion to her in her house. He has been here countless times, but he cannot help but stare in amazement every time he walks in.

A wall in her living room is covered by dozens of figurines and photographs: the Virgin Mary, Jesus Christ, the Twelve Apostles, and saints.

She takes small steps and opens the door to her room, which is decorated by many more saints. "People know I like them," Hernandez says. "They bring them to me and I keep them."

Alfonso sits besides her, holds her hand, and together they pray. He offers her a piece of the Host. She prays some more.

Alfonso tries to visit her every day.

Hope God Keeps Us Here

Religious brothers helped establish the Mission Queen of Angels in the Lehigh Valley in May 1998. Three arrived from Costa Rica to reach out to mostly Latino youths in the Allentown area, to form adult faith communities, and to assist the sick, elderly, and disabled.

The plan was to stay for just a few years, but their presence has been so welcomed by the community that they plan to stay indefinitely. "I hope God keeps us here for many years," Brother Isaac says.

At Sacred Heart Church at Fourth and Pine streets, where the missionaries center much of their work, more than half of the congregants are Latino, says Monsignor Joseph R. Sobiesiak, who was pastor of the church before being transferred elsewhere.

Bringing Hope

It's a weekday afternoon, a day Alfonso goes to Lehigh County Prison with the two other brothers who are staying at the mission. The entrance room feels so cold that he hugs himself for a few seconds. Something about the gray floor and walls makes him a little nervous.

The brothers go to different rooms to meet with prisoners. Alfonso shakes hands with the prisoners who file into an empty room that resembles a classroom. He smiles nervously and glances at the guard standing outside the room, a few feet away.

His desire to bring hope is stronger than any fears he has among the prisoners, he reminds himself almost every time he is here.

A bilingual prisoner volunteers to translate his words to the non-Spanish speakers.

"Jesus was a prisoner just like you," he tells the group of about fifteen men, some young, some middle-aged, some unshaven, with stains on their white T-shirts. They nod and stay quiet, waiting to hear what he has to say.

The man repeats his words in English and Alfonso nods his head, agreeing with every word, as if he understood him. Alfonso also offers Bible studies to those who want to attend during their recreational hour.

One of the prisoners says that he has read the Bible many times but does not understand what he reads. People need to find themselves in the book, Alfonso tells him in Spanish.

About an hour later, as the prisoners get up to leave, they shake his hand and call him "Father." He could correct them and say, no, no, I'm just a religious brother, not a father yet. But he refrains, smiling. He likes the sound of the word "father." He does look like a priest, after all, wearing his gray robe that covers his feet and the wooden cross around his neck.

Other prisoners thank Alfonso for remembering them, for bringing them hope for the future.

Remember to Smile

Between his visits, Alfonso says, he finds time to have fun. Not all is spiritual service. He goes to the park with youths he ministers. He inline skates and enjoys cookouts. He also has a sense of humor.

"People forget that we are humans too," he says.

He walks toward his house and passes another church, Emmanuel Assembly of God. "The competition," he says jokingly.

He greets people along the way. He seems happy. People are surrounded by tragic images—wars, hurricanes, poverty, sickness—so often that they need to be reminded to smile.

At the end of the day, Alfonso has time to reflect on his life. He wishes more people were helping him minister to Latinos.

He tries not to think too much about it. It would frustrate him even more. All he can do is lead by example, hoping to find another sixteen-year-old who, like him, would be enchanted by the life of a brother, sister, or priest.

He will find that youngster one day, he reassures himself. For now, he is focusing on his goal: religious life.

"I don't regret my decision," he says. "It is hard sometimes. But I know I have made the right decision."

DOWN TO BUSINESS

On any day, you can find Jong Kim behind the counter of his clothing store, scanning his Korean-Spanish language dictionary. He comes across a Spanish word he has not seen before—*enfermo*, which means sick—and then finds the Korean translation.

He then repeats some letters of the Spanish alphabet out loud to practice their pronunciation.

"That's very good," says Alejandro Hernandez, manager of Kim's store, Parks.

Kim is speaking Spanish better every day. Since his Hamilton Street clothing store is in a heavily Latino neighborhood in center-city Allentown, he can't avoid the Latino influence.

Kim has discovered what many other Asian business owners have in the past few years. Asian immigrants leave their country thinking that they will need English to survive in the American business world. But once they reach the United States, they find a version of America not all of them were ready for.

They settle in Latino enclaves and find themselves adapting not only to mainstream America, but also to the world of Latinos—the largest minority group in the Lehigh Valley.

"It is very important for Asian immigrants to adapt to the Latino culture," says H. Walker Lee, member and former board member of the Lehigh Valley Organization of Chinese Americans. "Almost everybody in this country needs to learn about other cultures. And being that Latinos make such a significant portion of the population, many Asians are learning about Latinos."

Immigrants have been making their way to the United States for generations. Many expect to live in an English-speaking world, but end up living among other immigrants.

During the early part of the last century, European immigrants came to America through Ellis Island in New York. The Lower East Side became known as "Little Germany" during the early 1900s.

Newer Irish and other European immigrants arrived there and began adapting not only to the American way of life, but also to that of the German Americans.

Many decades later, Asian immigrants are the ones arriving in Latino neighborhoods in the United States, primarily opening family-owned businesses as a means of survival. Many figure they are better off working long days and being their own bosses, Lee said.

Second-generation Asians tend to adapt to the mainstream much faster, he says, often going to college and working in corporate America.

Even though Asians are one of the smallest ethnic groups in the Lehigh Valley—about 2 percent in the region—they own half of all minority-owned businesses in the Allentown-Bethlehem-Easton metropolitan area.

It is common to hear Asian business owners in center-city Allentown saying "gracias" and "adios" instead of "thank you" and "goodbye." Recently, Wanda Villamidez, a resident of downtown Allentown, came to Parks looking for shoes. She only speaks Spanish.

Kim can direct customers to the *zapatos* (shoes) or *pantalones* (pants) aisles. But for more involved conversations, he requires the assistance of his store manager.

"I try to learn Spanish, but it is very complicated," he says. "You have to learn the Spanish [word], and then the Korean meaning, and then the English translation."

Because his Spanish is limited, he has hired Latino employees who speak Spanish and can draw nearby residents to the store.

"There will be many more Spanish than now," Kim says. "We need to learn about other cultures, not just one."

Hernandez quickly walks over to Villamidez and assists her in her search for shirts, pants, and shoes.

She walks to Lee's counter. Hernandez stands by in case Kim needs a translation. After living for more than a decade in Allentown, Kim has learned to adapt to the immigrant community. When he lived in Korea, he learned about the American way of life. He learned about the Civil War, the American flag, and the United States as a world superpower, but little about Latinos in America, he said.

Tammy Yam, a waitress for the family-owned House of Chen restaurant on Hamilton Street in Allentown, had a similar experience.

While living in Malaysia, Yam used to watch American movies and television shows, where she saw light-skinned men and women speaking English. That was the America she pictured, and she began taking English classes to prepare herself for life in the United States.

Four years ago, when Yam arrived in Allentown to work with her aunt, she found a slightly different version of the America she had seen on screen. The majority of her customers are Spanish-speaking Latinos.

"I still think everybody should speak English, but I also wish I knew more Spanish to communicate with my customers," Yam says. "We get by, though. I am learning many Spanish words."

Yam is catching up pretty quickly. On any given day, one can hear Yam speaking Spanish words to her customers.

"Fried chicken is a popular dish here," she says. "So, I know how to say 'pollo frito.'"

She has also picked up other Spanish words by talking to her co-worker Santos Sotos, a dishwasher.

"He taught me how to say '¿Que pasa aqui?' What is happening here?"

"She learns pretty quickly," Sotos says.

Yam's aunt and supervisor, Jenny Lim, has also found herself learning more Spanish to communicate better with her customers. Lim arrived from Malaysia in her teens and took four years of Spanish classes while at William Allen High School during the late 1970s.

Now, Lim will make sure her three school-aged children learn both Spanish and English so that they can function in the business world in center-city Allentown.

"I took Spanish classes because everybody else was taking them," Lim says. "I never knew how important it would become."

AIRWAVE WARS

The men and women sitting around this large table don't look happy. There is a radio playing in the background. That is, after all, what brought them here today. The radio. The Lehigh Valley has become a battleground for two big-city Spanish-language radio stations that are vying for the lion's share of morning listeners.

But shock jocks from both stations have upset these men and women, members of an elite group of Latino leaders. They are tired of the disc jockeys' crude jokes and sex-laced banter.

The seven committee members of the organization known as the Latin Alliance got together this day to draft a letter to the morning shows on La Mega, a station in Philadelphia, and La Rumba, in New York. No more stereotypes, they say.

"We just want people who work in the mass media to take their jobs seriously," said Elsa Vazquez, a member of the Latin Alliance, which represents more than a dozen Latino groups in the Lehigh Valley. "What they say can influence a lot of people."

Latino radio listeners have only two options in the Lehigh Valley.

English speakers can simply turn the dial if they don't like what they hear, said Guillermo Lopez, another member of the Alliance. Spanish speakers only have La Mega and La Rumba. They are the only Spanish-language stations in the Valley listed by Arbitron, which ranks stations by popularity among listeners.

Despite concerns over the content of the two morning shows, Latino leaders can't ignore their popularity among Latino listeners.

La Mega's morning show on channel 1320 AM, with disc jockeys John Musa and VJ Mar, is the most popular show in La Mega's history and has helped increase the overall ratings of the station, radio executives admit.

La Rumba, on channel 107.1 FM, is broadcast from New York but has a satellite office in East Stroudsburg, near Allentown. Though its ratings aren't as high as La Mega's, it is trying to win over listeners with chatter and raunchy material.

Morning show disc jockeys from both stations said their antics are pure fun. La Mega's morning show hosts said that the women who call or visit the station to expose parts of their bodies participate freely. They also say that critics focus solely on the edgy and sexually explicit jokes and dismiss the public service work the hosts do.

"If you find the morning show offensive, turn it off and please come back after 10 a.m., because we have other not-so-offensive shows," said Karl Douglass, La Mega's director of sales. "The truth is we are a business, and we are rating reliant. Our ratings have gone to the roof with the morning show."

Besides "acting silly on air," La Mega disc jockeys Musa and Mar said they have helped people find jobs and a lost loved one, gotten a wheelchair for a person in need, and have participated in charity events.

"It's like the good things we do don't count at all," said Mar, also known as Victor Martinez, a co-host and director of La Mega. "It's the edgy stuff that sticks on their minds."

La Rumba disc jockeys said they could be raunchier if they wanted, like other radio stations, but they don't want to seem like copycats.

"We are just ourselves," said La Rumba's morning show host Jimmy Nieves.

On this morning, La Mega's morning show hosts broadcast live from Allentown, instead of Philadelphia, to be closer to fans in the Lehigh Valley. Throughout the morning, fans visited the station's office near Lehigh Valley International Airport.

Friends Leslie Vega and Evelyn Oqueda, both of Allentown, waited in line to meet celebrity disc jockeys Musa and Mar.

The morning show had been losing listeners when its content revolved around community news and serious matters. Station executives then decided to team up their two most popular disc jockeys and give them free rein in the morning. The pairing made both of them celebrities.

"Our ratings were really low," Martinez said. "People have enough problems at home and work, and they want a moment where they can laugh from their houses to their way to work. They deserve at least a little time of just silly fun."

The formula paid off.

"Every morning I tune in to hear what crazy stuff they have to say," Vega said. "It's silly, sometimes stupid stuff, but it's funny."

"It makes me laugh," Oqueda said.

Every morning Musa has plenty of material he knows his fans will enjoy.

"I'm a simple man," he said. "I like coffee, sex, and beans."

On this day, his material includes a calendar of nude women, which he plans to describe on the air.

"It looks like somebody poured a piece of meat on this woman," he says, describing one picture on the calendar. "We want to see Allentown breasts and see if they are different [from Philadelphia's]."

That gets the callers started. A young Allentown woman calls to tell them she is so attractive, "like Jennifer Lopez," that men are afraid to approach her. The disc jockeys ask young men to show up at the station so that the woman can pick a date.

She comes to the office, and an hour later a man in his early twenties shows up and she leaves with him. A few minutes later, a caller tells the disc jockeys that the woman was married and her husband had gone to pick her up.

"She was married!" Musa exclaims.

"Don't do anything stupid," he tells the apparent husband over the radio. "She was just having fun. No harm done."

The morning host, people in the studio, and the callers all laugh. This, after all, is a typical day on the Musa and Mar morning show. To stay on top of the ratings, the disc jockeys must give their listeners what they want, radio executives said.

On a different morning, the three disc jockeys for La Rumba's Big City Radio gear up to try to win some of La Mega's listeners in the New York and Pennsylvania area.

It's not an easy task, but they are up to the challenge, they say. Disc jockeys Rosemary "Boquita" Almonte, Emy Pena, and Jimmy Nieves want to create a "show that is different," and they're not afraid to tell listeners that La Rumba is the underdog.

"Coming up this hour we have big money prizes?" asks Nieves on the radio.

"NNNNNNNNNNNNOOOOOOOO," yell Almonte and Pena.

"We have big celebrities?"

"NNNNNNNNOOOOOOOO."

What they have is their sense of humor and a clash of personalities. Nieves is usually the one with the sexually explicit jokes and crude language. Pena tries to tone down his comments, and Almonte describes herself as someone in the middle.

During the show, Nieves tells the other hosts on the air that he went to the store to buy a new doll from the Disney movie *Lilo & Stitch*.

"But Lilo is so sexy that when my wife and daughter went to the store, I took the doll to the room," Nieves jokes.

Pena shouts back right away, "He is making movies for little kids into porn. That's not right, Jimmy!"

But they all laugh, knowing it was a joke—edgy, but funny, they say.

"Our show is just like a conversation between friends, but on air," Nieves said. "We could be worse. There are radio stations that set up scenarios and have people calling with weird situations. We don't like doing that."

They do get in trouble sometimes, they admitted. Alberto "El Ambon" Huerta's job is to go out on the streets and do practical jokes. On this day, the radio personality carries a sign that reads, "I suck. Yell at me for a dollar."

"I want to help people relieve their stress," El Ambon says. He talks to several people and finally finds a person to yell at him.

"Ridiculous!" the man yells.

"Sometimes I do get people angry," El Ambon says, "but it's fun."

Some area Latino leaders say they don't appreciate the stations' idea of fun.

The leaders are concerned because children can easily turn on the radio and listen. Even adult Latinos have few options in the morning.

Felix Molina, a member of the Puerto Rican Cultural Alliance, said that while he was taking a group of children on a field trip recently, he turned on the radio and the children listened to some of La Mega's morning show. Soon, the young-sters were imitating the bad behavior and language from the hosts.

"I told them, 'Don't say that,' and they would tell me, 'Why is it bad to say bad words if they are saying them on the radio?'" Molina said. "What do you say to that?"

Rafael Canizares, executive director of Latinos for Healthy Communities, said he often hesitates over whether to advertise notices about disease prevention on radio stations that use strong sexual content and vulgarity to increase ratings.

"I am trying to educate people about diseases and serious topics, and yet some of their shows have questionable content," Canizares says. "I have to really think about it before I advertise to them."

Radio profanity is not exclusive to Spanish-language radio. More mainstream celebrities, such as Howard Stern, who air sexually explicit and offensive material have been fined thousands of dollars by the Federal Communications Commission.

"We know that they will probably not tone down what they say," Lopez, the Alliance member, reflects, "but they have to know how some people in the Lehigh Valley feel."

GOOOAAALLL!!!

Juan Carlos Moreno gets impatient as he watches the group of men try to work the soccer ball down the field.

They lose the ball, get it back, lose it.

Moreno shakes his head, takes his cap off, puts it back on. It does not look good, he says, not good.

His team of soccer players, Deportivo Colorines, runs from one side of the field to the other, constantly losing the soccer ball to members of the "American" team, Kwik Goal.

This is not just another Sunday at the park. This is *futbol*, Spanish for soccer, a sport that runs in the blood of many Latin Americans.

"This is our sport," says Alonzo Gallego, president of the Lehigh Valley Latin Soccer League. "Latinos have a passion for futbol like no one else."

Soccer is for Latinos what baseball is for Americans: the national sport.

But visitors to some of the Latin League games, usually at Saucon Park in Bethlehem, can see that futbol is not just for Latinos.

For one of the games, some American players who do not understand much Spanish take the field. They nod to the Mexican players and begin kicking the ball.

Some of the "Anglo" players say they do not regret trading their all-American sport for soccer. Not only do they get to learn new athletic skills, but they also experience a new culture and socialize, at least for one day of the week, with a different ethnic group, says Bruce Hirthler, a Kwik Goal player.

"It does not matter what nationality you are or what language you speak on the soccer field," Hirthler says. "I can almost know what they are saying. I don't understand the language, but I understand the game, and that's the language we all speak."

The Latin League welcomed its first non-Latino team a few years ago when Kwik Goal joined. Ever since, the team has held its own.

This year, the league welcomed Pac Wilcox, a team sponsored by Portuguese Lehigh Valley residents. The Anglos have played against local teams with players from Ecuador, Colombia, Honduras, Peru, and other countries.

The sad truth is, Hirthler says, Latinos and Anglos rarely get together—except on the soccer field.

On this Sunday, Kwik Goal faces a team made up mostly of immigrants from Estado de Mexico in Mexico. The American team has fifteen Anglos and five Latinos.

So far, the Americans have scored a goal. Lucky shot, says Moreno, the coach of Deportivo Colorines—Spanish for "the colorful sportsmen."

The Mexicans will overcome. After all, many team members have played futbol ever since "we were this big," Moreno says, raising his hand to the height of his waist.

"Our team is also pretty new," Moreno says. "This is our second season playing. Our players are just getting used to each other."

On the other side of the field, Juan Vinces, a middle-aged native of Peru, keeps a close watch on the Kwik Goal players in blue. Most of his team members began playing in high school or later.

He knows that the team of Mexicans, like most Latino players, were kicking a soccer ball as soon as they could walk.

"I tell you something: Americans are fast," Vinces says. "They run very fast, but this is not a sport of speed.

"It's about taking control of the ball, keeping the ball," he says. "You only use speed when you really need it."

Knowing this, he decided to add some Latino players to his mostly Anglo team. The Latino players teach the Anglo players how to take control of the ball. When you add control and speed, you have a powerful combination, he says.

Some Mexican team members look worried. One of their team members gets the ball and stops for a few seconds.

"What are you waiting for, to have your picture taken?" some people in the stand yell in Spanish. "Kick that ball!"

Moreno says futbol is more than the game on the field. His team members play to remember their roots, to keep their tradition alive, to socialize with friends, to have the moms and the sisters cheering in the back, to have their children imitate them in an open space behind the field.

On the other side of the field, Hirthler takes a break. He would not be here if it weren't for his high school friend Cesar Vinces, the coach's son.

Vinces persuaded Hirthler to return to soccer seven years after they last played together.

Playing soccer has helped Hirthler escape the suburban atmosphere of Perkiomenville for a day and interact with his new Spanish-speaking friends.

"Latinos play very differently," he says. "You get to learn how they play their way and you do well."

One of the Mexican players, Jose Salguero, of Allentown, glances at his watch. There are only a few minutes before the game ends, and the Americans have already scored two more goals.

"I do not think we can win this game anymore," Salguero says. "I am hoping at least we can tie the game."

One of the game organizers blows his whistle and raises a flag. Game over.

"I can't believe it!" Salguero says. "Not a single goal."

"If we cannot beat the Americans, it is going to be much more difficult to beat the Central Americans next week," Moreno tells a few team members standing near him. "It is back to practice, guys, this Tuesday."

Gustavo Santana walks toward Moreno and smiles gently. Their relatives stand behind the team members, some smiling, others chatting, but none of them look sad.

After a few seconds, the team members walk toward their loved ones. Tomorrow will mean going back to the same routine: work and school for most.

But at least, some of the players say, they had their Sunday of futbol, and they got to share it with the Anglos.

"We lost," Santana tells Moreno, "but it was a good game."

UNFULFILLED DREAMS

They knew each other in Honduras, but after coming to the United States, they discovered a bond that gave them strength and comfort.

Aneht Argueta arrived first in the Lehigh Valley, in December 1999, to find work. Her aunt, Naomi Eda Zelaya, arrived in July 2001. Separately they had crossed three borders, risking the chance of rape and even death.

Argueta provided immediate refuge for the newer immigrant. Zelaya's accents, mannerisms, and customs triggered memories of the homeland that her niece sorely missed.

In a year's time, Argueta would teach her aunt, who was not yet in the country legally, how to survive as an immigrant in the United States.

Zelaya, in turn, would teach Argueta about the value of friendship. But a bigger lesson, about not taking life for granted, would come in August 2002, when Zelaya was struck by a car and killed.

The relationship between the women is not unlike those of most immigrants, who depend on friendships for moral and economic support. Newcomers, particularly those who are not yet legal, usually don't have jobs or a place to stay.

Once here, fellow immigrants, usually from the same country of origin, provide shelter and help in finding jobs and a network of other immigrants. All they have is each other.

A Bond Forms

The bond between the women, despite a twelve-year age difference, began to take hold in July 2001.

Zelaya arrived in the Easton area that month by bus. She brought no luggage. Then thirty-six, she carried only a piece of paper, tucked in a pocket of her white jeans. On it was written her niece's name and address.

Not knowing Argueta's apartment number, Zelaya sat on a sidewalk outside the apartment complex, waiting for Argueta to come out. Eventually, Argueta, then twenty-four, looked out her second-story apartment and saw her aunt. She was surprised, believing that Zelaya, after a year of trying, had given up on crossing into the United States through Mexico.

Argueta rushed downstairs. The women hugged and cried.

Argueta had left behind a son in Honduras. Zelaya had left behind five children with her husband.

"I miss my children so," Argueta remembers Zelaya telling her. "But I have to do this."

Though men cross the border more frequently, it's not uncommon for women to immigrate alone, particularly if they're single or their spouses are unable to work. Zelaya planned to work in the Lehigh Valley for a short time, sending money back home to her family to build a new house and finance her children's education. She wanted to move back eventually, possibly by the end of 2002.

"My husband is sick," she told Argueta. "I am the one who has to work."

Argueta was seven years old when the two first met in Honduras. Zelaya had defied her parents by eloping with Argueta's uncle, Edgardo, at nineteen. She went to live under the same roof with Argueta.

A few days later, Argueta stood in a corner as Zelaya rushed into the bathroom of the house, hiding from her grandmother, who was angry over the elopement.

Argueta did not say anything at the time, but she admired Zelaya for her courage in enduring hardships to be with the man she loved.

After Zelaya gave birth to her third son, she and her husband moved into their own house outside Saba Colon, Honduras. Argueta and Zelaya saw each other less and less. "We had our own lives," Argueta said.

Years later, Argueta better understood what Zelaya had gone through. She met a guy and later had a son, Humberto. At twenty-two, pregnant, she left Honduras for the Lehigh Valley, where her sister was living.

When Zelaya arrived in the Valley two years later, she felt somewhat lost. America was a big land filled with people who did not speak her language, said her husband, Edgardo Hernandez, in a phone interview from Honduras.

Argueta is your link to that world, he reminded her.

By then, Argueta knew the ins and outs of immigrant life in the Valley. She had worked in area factories and helped her aunt meet other immigrants who knew of job openings. She also let Zelaya live with her and her boyfriend for a few months.

In a matter of weeks, it seemed as though the two women had long been best friends.

Argueta took Zelaya shopping, gave her rides to work, showed her around. She explained that in the United States, everyone has rights. Argueta had a book about the rights of immigrants in the United States and often quoted from it.

"Don't ever let anyone treat you like you are less than human," she told Zelaya. "Some employers take advantage of that. Here, everyone is a person."

It took a while, but Zelaya began to understand this. After working ten-hour shifts at area factories, she found a job with better hours through her immigrant contacts. It was with Garex Systems Corp. in Allentown, a cleaning agency.

Though Zelaya had crossed the border illegally, she showed Garex Systems the documents, such as a Social Security card, that she needed to work legally in the United States, said her supervisor, Daniel Senece.

To be closer to her job, Zelaya moved to Allentown, sharing an apartment with another immigrant. "This will always be your house," Argueta told her when Zelaya left. "You leave because you want to."

But Argueta understood that her aunt needed to leave to improve herself.

"We always talked about how to better ourselves," Argueta said.

Zelaya explored other sides of her personality while living in the Valley. She had been conservative in Honduras, wearing long skirts and rarely attending dances. Here, she often danced to *punta* (Hondurans' traditional music), told jokes, and laughed for hours at her niece's place. She dressed more casually.

"We have to do it, like the clown who has to perform in front of a crowd even though his heart is bleeding," Zelaya, missing her family, would tell her niece.

Both women shared stories about how they managed to sneak into the United States. Zelaya, after leaving Honduras in May 1999, spent a year in Mexico City working odd jobs to make enough money to cross the border. At the border, bandits kidnapped her, hoping to get money from her relatives in the United States, her husband said.

But Zelaya would not tell her kidnappers she had relatives in America. After forty-six days in captivity, she escaped through a window and hired a "coyote," an illegal smuggler, to cross her over the Rio Grande. She paid $5,000.

"I pleaded with her to not go by herself to the United States," said her husband. "I knew how risky it was to cross. Losing your life is not worth searching for a better life, I told her. But she felt she had to go, for our children."

Argueta had gone through her own ordeal to reach the United States. While knowing she was pregnant, she hid for a day in the bottom luggage section of a bus to evade Mexican immigration officers as she crossed from Guatemala to Mexico.

About three months later, when she arrived in the Bethlehem area, where her older sister lived at the time, she was severely dehydrated.

She spent a few weeks at St. Luke's Hospital in Fountain Hill until she had energy to walk again. Social worker Janet Perez—"an angel," she says—helped her find grants to pay her medical bills.

She delivered a healthy baby boy, Ronald, a few months later.

Living together, Zelaya and Argueta wanted to focus on the future and made the best of their time together.

Argueta remembered when Ronald celebrated his first birthday, on July 31, 2001. She and Zelaya bought a cake and sodas to celebrate and invited the neighbors. Argueta could see the tears in Zelaya's eyes; Zelaya was missing her own children back in Honduras.

But they knew their children were the reason they were in the United States. Argueta, who works at a packing company, and Zelaya each tried to send about $150 or more a month back to their families. Argueta has a work permit to live in the United States. She checks with immigration officials periodically to keep her documents active.

Zelaya was learning English to get a better job. She bought books and watched television to pick up the language.

Zelaya would call home to Honduras, but would hang up right away. Her children's voices always made her weak in the knees.

"When are you coming home, Mommy?" her children would ask.

"I'm coming home soon," she would tell them. "Very soon."

A Life Cut Short

Living on Washington Street in Allentown, Zelaya usually got a ride to her job—cleaning offices at Agere Systems in Allentown—from her roommate, Pedro Torres. When his work schedule changed, she took the bus.

On August 13, she got off at her stop near the 500 block of Union Boulevard. Without the right of way, she began to cross the street and was struck by a car.

Finding a list of phone numbers in Zelaya's purse, officials at St. Luke's Hospital in Fountain Hill tried to reach Argueta, but she had recently changed her number. They contacted Zelaya's husband in Honduras, who eventually reached Argueta's sister in New Jersey.

It wasn't until the next morning that Argueta got the call from her sister and headed to the hospital.

Maybe Zelaya has a broken leg, Argueta told herself. I'm going to make her laugh, crack some jokes so she can feel better, she thought. At the hospital's front desk, and with her limited English, she asked for her aunt's room number—13, Intensive Therapy.

Argueta did not understand much English, but when she talked to a doctor, she understood the word "died." The news shocked her. Her aunt had died just before she arrived, at 6:56 a.m. that August 14.

Argueta broke down in tears. How could this happen? Asked by a doctor to identify Zelaya, she had to find the courage to do so.

When the shock receded, Argueta began thinking about her dreams, questioning whether it had been worth taking the risks to get to America. Zelaya's dreams died with her. Please, God, do not let me find the same ending, she prayed.

Zelaya's church, Iglesia Sinai on Second Street in Allentown, held a funeral service a few days later. Pastor Andres Rosa said she was well liked by the congregation.

Friends, family, and co-workers helped raise the $3,000 to send Zelaya's body back home. A week after the death, the casket arrived in Saba Colon. Zelaya's husband and children held a memorial service at their home. They held each other and cried.

The new house that Zelaya was helping pay for remains unfinished. The empty frame still needs doors, windows, and paint.

Now Argueta feels a more urgent desire to return to Honduras, if not for her, for the son she left behind, and in Zelaya's memory.

But she is afraid she'll never reunite with her family. Some mornings she wakes up and cries as she prepares lunch for the ten-hour workday ahead. She is worried she might die, as Zelaya did, before fulfilling her dreams.

With Zelaya's death, she learned not to take life for granted, that being in America, land of opportunity, does not mean she made it.

"We always talked about death. I used to joke with her and tell her, 'If you die, I'm not going to send your body back home.' I would say that because I knew how much she wanted to go back. They were just jokes, playing around. I regret saying that."

Now, every time Argueta calls her six-year-old son in Honduras, he tells her, "Mom, be careful. I don't want you to die like Edgardito's mother." (Edgardito is one of Zelaya's sons.)

"I will be careful," she tells him. "It will be all OK."

27

A RICH LIFE

Your name is on a guest list to visit the Ortiz family of East Stroudsburg. Once you arrive at the Penn Estates subdivision, you have to check in with the security guard at the gate and give your name, make of car, and license plate number.

The gates open. You drive another mile or so and admire the view. You park outside a two-story house surrounded by trees and mountain ridges.

Most Latino families in Pennsylvania—and the rest of the country—can't afford to live in an upscale subdivision with a security system like the Ortizes, judging from U.S. Census income data. Latinos in most parts of the state tend to be newcomers, earning a median income of $26,930.

But Monroe County is not like the rest of the state.

Here the median Latino income is $53,000, higher than the county's overall median income of $46,000.

The county's proximity to New York and its lower housing costs have turned the region into a Latino middle-class haven. Latinos can afford to live in upscale subdivisions in the Poconos and keep their jobs in the city, seventy-five miles away, said Jesus Sanchez, president of the Latino American Alliance of Monroe County.

"The Latinos who come here are professionals, people who want to enjoy a middle-class lifestyle in the suburbs," Sanchez said.

A three-bedroom, 1,800-square-foot house with a one-car garage costs $93,000 to $95,000 in the Pocono Mountains region, said Thomas Wilkins, president of Wilkins and Associates Real Estate. Similar square footage in New York City can cost between $200,000 and $300,000 (or more in Manhattan).

"About 70 percent of our buyers are what we typically call commuters from New York or New Jersey," Wilkins said. "They pay two to three times as much in New York. They get more for their money here."

In ten years, many Latino families, such as the Ortizes, have been lured to Monroe County. Latinos now make up about 7 percent of the county's population, compared with roughly 2 percent in 1990.

Despite the widespread belief that Latinos tend to be mostly low income, many are climbing the economic ladder, according to a Tomas Rivera Policy Institute analysis titled "The Latino Middle Class: Myth, Reality, and Potential." The institute researches issues affecting U.S. Hispanics. Its study found that more than one million Hispanic households joined the ranks of the middle class in the past two decades. U.S.-born Hispanics tend to make $40,000 or more a year, about twice as much as Latino immigrants earn.

The Ortizes have so many Latino neighbors that some Latino leaders call the subdivision where he lives "Latino Estates." Every year in early December the subdivision holds a Latin night to celebrate diversity in the community.

But living in Monroe County and working out of the state means a long commute.

"It's not an easy life, leaving before the sun comes out and coming home at dark," said Mike Ortiz, who travels by bus to New York for his job with AMC Corporation, a computer services company. "But offering my family a nice home in a safe place makes it worth it."

The Ortiz family moved to the Poconos in 1996 after a friend told Mike about the region. He liked the quiet atmosphere. He also liked the cost of living. He bought a house for his family, and a year later, one for his mother. In addition to his family's mortgage, he pays part of his mother's mortgage.

"It's tough, but you sacrifice other aspects of life, like vacationing, to make the payments," he said.

Most weekdays Ortiz wakes at 5 a.m. as his wife, Maria, and two-year-old son, Mateo, sleep.

"I wanted to propose to my girlfriend, only not until I had a house, something to offer her," he said. "I wanted to buy a house for both my mother and myself. I realized I could do that when I found Monroe County."

Said Maria, "I told him that if we were going to move to the mountains, I at least wanted some neighbors. It's a big change coming from the city. Sometimes I do miss the noise and fast-paced lifestyle, but I like the quiet too."

At the bus station, Ortiz meets up with friends Wilfredo and Marta Almanza, who also live in Penn Estates, and others.

It's a two-hour bus ride to his job at AMC, where he is a manager and earns $80,000 a year.

His friends also work in New York, but at hotels. Wilfredo Almanza is an engineer coordinator and his wife is an assistant controller. Both earn more than $40,000 a year.

When the Almanzas, who lived in the Bronx, moved to Penn Estates in 2000, the subdivision was not that developed.

Two years later the Almanzas are surrounded by neighbors, mostly Latinos from New York.

"We chose to move to the suburbs because we were after a quiet life," Almanza said. "We [Latinos] are multiplying here. In the last few years I have seen many Latinos move from New York to Monroe County. Everybody else wants the same thing."

Ortiz agrees. He said salaries of $40,000 to $80,000 "would be OK money in New York, but that money goes a long way in Pennsylvania."

Prosperity is the first step in becoming part of the power structure in the area, Sanchez, the local Latino American Alliance leader, said.

Latinos are still relatively new to this part of Pennsylvania, said Maria Roman Perez, a member of the Alliance. The community needs some time to adjust and start getting more involved as municipal and county leaders.

Sanchez has seen signs of that. He has seen professionals join the Latino American Alliance over the past few years, wanting to help fellow Latinos and the rest of the community.

"Latinos are doing well here," he said. "Now we want to get them more involved in politics."

28

LIBERTY AND JUSTICE FOR ALL

In the history books she read years ago, Maria Vazquez would see flags with lots of stars and red and white stripes.

She was not sure what the symbols meant. She saw pictures of older men wearing white wigs. The captions read, "founding fathers." She tried to read more, but did not understand most of the English words.

Even as a young girl, she wanted to immerse herself in American history and culture so she could become a citizen of the United States. For many years, she tried to learn.

"I read and read history books, but the information does not stick with me," she said in Spanish. "But I do know something—that this is the best country in the world."

Every Fourth of July, Americans take a day to commemorate the birthday of the United States. For many whose families have been here for decades, if not centuries, the holiday means patriotic displays and grand speeches about freedom.

But the holiday has not always had the same meaning for many people of color, especially those working hard for their piece of the American pie.

As these new Americans prosper, they equate the holiday with the founding of their own freedom and the opportunity to pursue their happiness. For some nonwhite Americans, the Fourth of July is a holiday of contradictions. Even though the U.S. Census shows the Lehigh Valley (and America at large) is more diverse than ever, its people are still not equal, some feel.

Latinos and African Americans still tend to be poorer than whites, the census shows. Latinos and African Americans also suffer disproportionately from diabetes, breast cancer, AIDS, and other diseases. Poverty means less access to health care, and that usually increases a person's likelihood of suffering from a disease, according to the National Hispanic Medical Association.

"These groups have been essentially excluded from better opportunities to become part of mainstream America," said Bill Scott, a professor of African American and African history at Lehigh University. "The real freedom for minority groups has not been realized up to this date."

But some see progress. "I think Latinos are feeling more ownership of this country," said Rafael Collazo of the U.S. Hispanic Leadership Institute, which works to get more Latinos involved in politics. "We are not moving back to our lands and are taking care of our destiny in the U.S. A number of us are joining the military. Family members have participated in wars. I see more and more pride."

Signs of progress include education, a category in which minorities are doing better than ever. According to the latest education report from the census, one-half of Asians and Pacific Islanders ages twenty-five to twenty-nine had earned a bachelor's degree or higher. About one in three whites graduated from college in the same age group, compared to about one in seven African Americans and one in ten Latinos in that age group. And as educational attainment grows, so does the quality of life, said Lehigh University's Scott.

But the statistics can be deceiving. "For the untrained eye, this is probably the best of times," Scott said. "But for the individuals without marketable skills, this is the worst of times."

Kevin Easterling, who works for the Alliance for Building Communities in Allentown, said he has had trouble feeling like a proud American every Fourth of July.

He began his self-discovery in college and found little about African American history in his textbooks. "There was almost no information that had to do with black people," he said. "We weren't free and that stuck in my head."

He began researching what it means to be a black American and came across a declaration written by an African American political activist of the 1800s, Frederick Douglass.

He read about and tried to picture himself in Douglass's shoes when Douglass addressed residents of Rochester, New York, at a Fourth of July celebration in 1852. He talked about the injustice of considering a black person three-fifths of a human being, of purchasing a black person for money, and of forcing blacks to work in inhumane conditions. And at a meeting of the American Anti-Slavery Society a few years before, Douglass had said, "I have no love for America, as such; I have no patriotism; I have no country."

The words were strong and powerful, Easterling remembers. Then he understood his own interpretation of the Fourth of July holiday—a dream for them, the European settlers.

"We did not come to the island [Ellis Island] like many immigrants," he said. "We were brought here."

Though Easterling recognizes that life has improved for many African Americans since the times of slavery and the civil rights movement, he said young African Americans should reconnect with their history and do better than their elders by going to college and becoming political leaders.

An increased interest in politics is also important for the Latino community. Collazo said that as the number of Latinos has grown in the country, so has the number of Latino leaders.

"We work, pay taxes, and do everything else Americans do," he said. "But we see people in power who speak and look different than us. We now live in a neighborhood that is changing."

Collazo said more Latinos will run for office, come out to vote, run school districts, join the armed forces, and gain political and cultural power.

"It's about time that we begin to see issues through brown eyes, too," he said. "That is how we can all celebrate Fourth of July, real freedom for all."

For Vazquez, in her mid-forties, these words cannot ring more true. Vazquez left her native Mexico two decades ago, planning to save some money and buy a house. Now she finds herself living the American dream, with three children and a husband who is in the Marine Corps.

"My life has not been easy, but I like my life very much right now," she said. "One day I will become an American citizen."

But now that she has the ideal American family—her oldest boy following his father into the Marines and a spacious home in Whitehall Township—Vazquez will once again start from scratch.

She will say goodbye to her adopted homeland and follow her husband, who has been reassigned to Japan.

"When you first get here, you don't want to be here," Vazquez said. "Now, all I want to do is stay here. This is my country now. I want to come back to it."

29

MAN OF THE CROSS

Weekdays, Alejandro Rodriguez, in his late twenties, works in a meatpacking plant in Souderton. But on this Good Friday in center-city Allentown, he portrayed Jesus Christ in a reenactment of Jesus's death walk and crucifixion that was so real some people could not hold back tears.

"Just seeing what he is going through and that he is being beaten makes it seem so real," said Viviana Cruz, who lives in nearby Easton. She followed the hour-long procession along Sixth and Gordon streets in the heart of downtown Allentown. "I cannot help but cry."

Hundreds walked along the route, which began at Sixth and Turner streets, in observance of Good Friday. The annual procession, which spanned about six city blocks, was organized by members of Sacred Heart Church on North Fourth Street, the church with the most Latino congregants in northeastern Pennsylvania.

Church members, who began practicing six weeks before the event, acted out the roles of Roman soldiers, Jesus's mother, Mary, and the dozens of disciples who had stayed with Jesus through his ordeal. The Stations of the Cross were narrated in Spanish.

Christians throughout the Lehigh Valley, as in many other places, observe Jesus's suffering by participating in cross carryings and attending church services that set the stage for the celebration of Easter Sunday.

Rodriguez, who moved to Allentown in 2000 after emigrating from Mexico, said he never saw himself playing Jesus in the reenactment. He began attending services at the church shortly after moving to the city and just wanted to attend Mass and activity groups. But Sister Isabel Sell, who helped organize the procession, insisted that he would be perfect to play the role of Jesus.

"I did not feel holy enough to play such a big character," Rodriguez said. "But the sister kept asking."

Finally, Rodriguez, who is slender and about five foot five, let his beard grow for about four weeks. His hair was already beyond shoulder length. All he needed to do was practice his role.

The crowd followed him along Gordon Street as he carried a seven-foot wooden cross on his shoulders. As he tried to walk, he fell several times along the route back to Sacred Heart Church.

Behind him, Jorge Nieves, who at six feet tall and 230 pounds played a Roman soldier, beat Rodriguez's back with a whip—slap! slap! one, two, three times—and demanded that he get up and carry the cross once again. Rodriguez stumbled to get up and followed his orders.

Nieves beat him again—slap! slap! slap! slap!—four times this time, then laughed and pointed his finger at him, making fun of his weakness.

Some of the residents along Gordon Street came out of their houses to investigate all the commotion. Monsignor Joseph Sobiesiak nodded and sighed in relief in having attracted people's attention.

"We chose this area because we felt some people here needed to see this, whether it has any effect on them or not," Sobiesiak said.

The procession ended at Sacred Heart Church, where Rodriguez was stripped of his handmade costume and symbolically nailed against the cross he had carried. In the background was the sound of hammering, to represent Jesus being nailed to the cross.

Juanita Pollock, who played Mary, held Rodriguez in her arms and cried, looking at his expressionless face and holding him tight. Her cries for the lost son were heard throughout the church. Many who watched wept even more.

Clouds of smoke and the sound of a thunderstorm, which played over the church's speakers, signified Jesus's death. Masses of people kneeled and cried as if Rodriguez had died in their presence.

Pollock said she could not help but cry real tears. When she held Rodriguez in her arms she thought about her son.

"I could not bear the thought of thinking of my son dying in my arms," Pollock said. "I cry the tears of a mother."

To conclude the service, some of the church members playing disciples carried an immobile Jesus covered by white blankets to another room.

Later, Rodriguez said he was happy that he had decided to participate in the live Stations of the Cross and play the role of Jesus.

"It was a unique experience," he said. "I'm just very tired."

30

FULL CIRCLE

Bartolo Figueroa walks with great effort onto his front porch, a crutch tucked under his left arm. He breathes heavily as he settles into a metal chair and stares out at the sea, only a block away.

He smells the salt air, carried by a warm breeze, and feels the burning sun warm his brown skin.

He enjoys the quiet.

Feels it.

At this stage in his life—in his seventies, heavyset, with advanced arthritis—he needs the quiet, he reassures himself.

"Do I miss Bethlehem?" he asks.

He shakes his head no.

Bethlehem was where Figueroa had followed legions of young men from Puerto Rico in the 1950s to work as a laborer at Bethlehem Steel. Like many men in Patillas, he grew sugarcane, but the island economy was poor. The mainland had a shortage of workers and the government was encouraging migration for its factories and farms.

Learning of the good-paying jobs by word of mouth, Figueroa left behind his wife, Santos, and four children, going to New Jersey briefly, and then Bethlehem, in the Lehigh Valley. He did some farm work before landing the job with Bethlehem Steel and sent home earnings. His intent was to return to the island within a few years.

He ended up staying for three decades in Bethlehem, known to the country as Christmas City.

He brought his family to the mainland, had four more children, and formed enduring friendships.

Still, Bethlehem never felt like home for him. He never forgot the promise he made to himself as a young man. "I was not going to leave Patillas forever," he recalls. So in the early 1980s, after retiring from Bethlehem Steel, he returned to Patillas with his wife, this time leaving his children and grandchildren behind in the Lehigh Valley.

"Many people from my town and others nearby made that same promise, to return, but not all did," Figueroa says. "It's not easy leaving your children and not seeing your grandchildren. But this was what I was going to do from the beginning."

Like Figueroa, other Steel retirees have returned to their native Puerto Rico, trading proximity to their extended families for the familiarity of their homeland.

Figueroa never owned a home in Bethlehem, only rented. He saved money to buy his first house—in Patillas.

"That was his dream," says his son, Daniel, who lives in Bethlehem.

Figueroa says he knows what retired life would be like for him had he stayed in Bethlehem. His children would go to work; the grandchildren, to school. He would be alone.

"Everybody is always so busy, and you stay indoors watching the television all day," he says. "And the weather, it gets so cold you cannot even move."

He had lived in Bethlehem long enough.

"I am from here," Figueroa says of Patillas. "And here is where I want to stay."

Miguel Marrero and Ernesto Colon, who also spent decades working at Bethlehem Steel, identify with Figueroa. Both were young when they left Puerto Rico for Bethlehem, where, with their wives, they raised their children. But they, too, longed for their homeland.

"You never forgot where you came from," says Colon, a Steel laborer for about thirty years.

Today, Colon also lives in Patillas with his wife in a modest one-bedroom house. Marrero, a native of Corozal, lives with his wife in a one-bedroom apartment in the island's largest city, San Juan.

"You go out in the streets, and you see people talking, walking. People live outdoors here," says Marrero, now in his sixties. "That is what I missed when I was in Bethlehem."

Marrero was a laborer at Steel, and later, a recruiter. After about twenty years, he moved back to Puerto Rico, at age forty-five. Today, he is a part-time real estate agent for mainland companies that want to open businesses on the island, such as Pep Boys, an auto supply store.

"It can be hectic at times," he says. "But it is still Puerto Rico."

Like Figueroa, Marrero and Colon have visited their children in the Lehigh Valley, and their children fly to the island to visit them.

Paradise with a Price

On this day in Patillas, Figueroa looks at the sun, and from its position in the sky, figures that it's midafternoon. He is not wearing a watch. He's getting hungry. He walks slowly inside his house and opens the refrigerator. Not much food. Water. A piece of bread. He feels his stomach growl.

Someone calls to him. "Bartolo!"

He turns to see his neighbor Genesis Pagano, a local third-grader who has become a loyal companion in the past few years. He smiles broadly.

"Come on in, *muchachita*," he says, welcoming her.

Figueroa enjoys the youngster's company.

With his children and grandchildren in the Lehigh Valley, and his wife deceased, he spends his time talking to neighbors, sitting on his porch, playing dominoes on the beach, or playing slot machines at the corner store late into the night.

"It makes time go faster," he'll tell you.

His bright green house near the beach is small, like others in the neighborhood. It has one bedroom, a small bathroom, and a kitchen. There is a lone sofa in the living room, a small color television, and a couple of stools in the kitchen. A nurse checks on him periodically. Lately he has not tended his backyard. His health keeps him from heavy activity, he says.

Now, the phone rings, and Figueroa moans in discontent.

"I'll get it," screams Genesis, and runs to his bedroom to pick it up.

"Who is it?"

"A person who is mute," she says. "Nobody answered."

Both laugh, and he pats her on the shoulder.

They agree to get lunch and slowly start the short walk to Calixto Place, a store at the end of his block. Figueroa moves his feet as if they weigh too much. Genesis walks around him and from side to side, but does not pass him. She knows Figueroa can't walk as fast as she can.

"Bartolo, we are almost there," she says.

Figueroa wants to reply, but has only energy to smile.

Smallville

Leave Patillas? Are you serious? Look around, Figueroa says to visitors. Patillas is like paradise.

The sentiment is shared by many in this town of twenty thousand in southeast Puerto Rico, about an hour and a half drive from San Juan.

Those who live by the beach wake up to the early sounds of birds, roosters, crashing waves, and children running around. Few of the locals are wealthy, and the majority live in modest one- or two-story bright-colored houses. The streets are paved, some so narrow—a car's width—that two neighbors can walk out of their homes and be face to face. In the region, people grow sugar and oranges or work in stores.

People know one another, but that is not always good, jokes produce vendor Pablo Rodriguez, who sells vegetables in an outdoor bodega.

"What are you now going on your fourth wife?" jokes a customer. "You have eight kids—and with different women."

"People here can tell you anything about each other," Rodriguez says, smiling at the customer. "People here are beautiful inside and out. I would never leave here." The town is also a safe haven, says police officer Carlos J. Soto Ayala. It is patrolled by about twenty-six officers. On this afternoon, about twelve officers on duty chat in the precinct headquarters break room. All is quiet. The town, says young officer Pena Colon, has not recorded a homicide in the two years he has been an officer.

"People just yell at each other," Colon says. "But it always stops at that."

There are two central churches in the town plaza: one Methodist, the other Catholic. People socialize in the plaza, especially after church gatherings. The town has mostly older residents and young children. Young adults leave to attend universities in the island's bigger cities. Or, like Carlos Manuel Estrada, in his early thirties, they go to the United States. Bethlehem and Allentown are familiar city names.

Estrada, like many young people in Figueroa's generation, heard of Bethlehem by word of mouth. He worked in a slaughterhouse near Bethlehem for three years but decided to move back to the island, where he became a police officer.

People earn more in the United States, Estrada says, but money goes further in Patillas. The average U.S. family earns about $42,000 a year. An average family in Puerto Rico earns about $26,000.

Estrada makes about $12,000 as a police officer, and pays about $200 a month for a one-bedroom apartment in Patillas. The average rent for one- and two-bedroom apartments in Bethlehem is at least $350 to $500.

"Money in Bethlehem was good, and I had made good friends," Estrada says. "But my family is here, and while I make less money here, this is where my wife is."

Others say they will never leave the island, no matter what idyllic picture people paint of the United States.

"People from here are always going to Allentown, Bethlehem, Lancaster and come back with money, they say. But what's the point if they are away from home?" asks Angel Lavoy, an island native in his mid-forties.

The Old Man and the Girl

Figueroa and Genesis arrive at Calixto Place, which has two pool tables and four slot machines. Figueroa orders empanadas—fried dough filled with meat and beans. Genesis doesn't order.

Genesis's mother, Wanda Vazquez, works at the store. She gives Figueroa a message: a delivery truck is dropping off his electric wheelchair. The driver had called the store when he did not find Figueroa at home.

It is in moments like this that Figueroa can take advantage of his life's work. He receives about $1,600 a month in Social Security and Bethlehem Steel pensions. He was able to buy his first house for $32,000 when he moved back to Patillas. Now he will kick in $1,200 for the electric wheelchair. Most of the cost, nearly $5,000, is paid by Medicaid.

By the time Figueroa gets back home, a white truck with the sign "CRE Rental Hospital Supplies" is waiting. Neighbors are curious. The delivery is big news in this small town.

He ordered the wheelchair to get around faster, he tells them.

"He really needs it," says neighbor Ramona Rivera, in her mid-fifties.

Genesis gives the chair a try without asking, riding it up and down the block. She screams when she nearly hits a pole in front of Figueroa's house. Figueroa chuckles.

After signing the needed paperwork and receiving instructions, it's Figueroa's turn. He settles into the wheelchair.

"Aaahh, this feels good," he says.

He plays with the speed control and rides back to the store over a paved but bumpy street to show off the wheelchair. Genesis runs behind him, laughing all the way.

"You are going to be faster than me, Bartolo," she says.

"You are going to be able to go all over town now," says Genesis's father, Efrain.

Figueroa stops the wheelchair briefly outside the store. He sees young people rush to the beach. He sees men his age playing dominoes. Many years have passed since he first left. People have come and gone. But Patillas maintained its essence— the easygoing lifestyle of his people.

"I worked so much and so hard throughout my life, and look at me now, how I ended," Figueroa says, holding back giggles. "In a wheelchair."

FINDING THE INNER SNOWMAN

I always wanted to write about Latinos, who tend to come from warm-weather countries, adapting to cold weather. But I never found the right angle. Then I realized that I am a Latino from a warm country—so my own experience became the angle I needed.

As a child I used to watch movies about children playing in the snow, building snowmen, and throwing snowballs at each other.

It looked as if those children lived in a fairyland. I wanted to be one of them so badly, but living in a desertlike climate in central Mexico, it seemed very unlikely.

Fast-forward thirteen years.

What was I thinking?

I mean, seriously. Living in a snow-prone area was nothing like what I had imagined. My honeymoon with snow was over. Let's see the divorce papers.

Being raised in Mexico and the southwest United States, I had only experienced snow by watching the Weather Channel and some Disney movies. So when I moved to Allentown in 2001, I had to admit, I was excited about seeing snow for the first time.

I waited and watched the local weather reports almost every night. Cold tomorrow and the next day, the TV weather guy would say. No snow yet. It was only October, after all.

Then, one day in December, unexpectedly, after waking up early to cover a 6 a.m. assignment, I glanced out the window to find snow. Wow. I looked around my mostly empty apartment and did not have anybody to share my enthusiasm with.

Oh, well, I said to myself, and walked outside. Entire roads and sidewalks were covered in snow. I was breathless for a few seconds. My center-city neighborhood in Allentown looked like the image of a shaken snow globe.

I walked toward my car, and that's when my hardships began. The snow looked pretty on the street, but boy, I did not want it on my car. Windshields, tires, doors, all covered in snow.

People at work had been telling me to "winterize"—buy a snow-brush, scraper, boots, and cat litter, in case my car gets stuck in the middle of a snowy road.

Did I listen? Not exactly. I had to grab a towel from the apartment and tried to get the snow off my windshield and doors. It was no big deal, really. I still was pretty happy about the snow, so I called my folks back in south Texas, where I lived until 1999.

"Is it snowing a lot over there in Nebraska?" my mother asked.

"No Mom, I live in Pennsylvania, but yes, it is snowing. Lots."

"Well, be careful," Mom said.

I hung up, and I realized that, like my folks, I was a little clueless about the snow. I went to a store and bought every other product that would protect me—shovel, scraper, giant brush, and so on.

No use.

Snowstorms followed, at least twelve inches in some parts of the city early that month, and no brush or cat litter could save me from the snow. During the last big snow, I tried driving the half mile to work. Not a good idea. I drove my car, and it took fifteen minutes to advance a few feet.

RRRrrrrrrr.

My car kept slipping when I attempted to go uphill, so I decided to drive downhill until I could find a street that was not as snow covered as the others. I drove toward one of the main roads, Hamilton Street, very slowly. Half an hour to cross a few blocks. I was not in a good mood.

At work, my supervisor said she needed to talk to me.

"I have a fun assignment for you," she said.

It better not involve snow, I told myself.

"It involves snow," she said.

She paired me with a photographer and asked us to find out how some people decided to spend their snow day.

Maybe it's not so bad, I told myself. Maybe I am going about this snow thing all wrong. There have to be people having a grand time, just like the people in the Disney movies I watched as a child.

A colleague had seen a group of children building snowmen at the corner of Sixteenth and Tilghman streets, and the photographer drove us there. Once again, I faced the snow.

Snowflakes began obstructing my view, covering my glasses every other second. My legs shook, because of the cold, I figured, even though I could not feel them. When I started writing, my pen didn't work because the ink was frozen.

The children seemed to be doing just fine and did not seem bothered by the constant snowfall. Hmm. I got closer and yes, the children seemed to be smiling.

I was intrigued.

The six youngsters looked at me. I looked at them. Some of them could not feel their hands. Their faces were red and their lips were about to turn purple.

"So, how, exactly, is all of this fun?" I asked them.

"Like hello? Building snowmen?" replied Tyisha Bell, thirteen, one of the children building a snow family. "It's a lot of fun."

The children seemed unaffected by the clogged streets, the snow shoveling, the fender benders, and other inconveniences. I took a pencil out of my backpack and began jotting down their uplifting comments. I thanked them and walked away.

After filing the story for the next day's paper, I found it impossible to drive back home. So, I walked, about twenty minutes nonstop, teeth chattering and all. It's in those moments that I miss the burning sun of south Texas, about nine miles from Mexico. As I walked home, I melancholically wondered whether I would ever get to wear T-shirts, shorts, and sandals again.

I watched the snow falling. The sky was so dark and beautiful and I could almost count the snowflakes. It looked pretty, magical even.

Maybe the children who built the snowmen were right. Maybe I was just being a little bit too negative about the snow. Their nine-foot snowman and the two smaller ones did look pretty neat.

Maybe I needed to find the inner child in me again. Maybe I needed to just let loose and have fun, to stop being the snow Grinch and just enjoy the darn season. Maybe that was what I needed, a bunch of hyper children to remind me to see the positive in not-so-ideal situations.

Maybe I could build a snowman. On second thought, that would involve my getting wet and cold just to create a snow figure that's going to melt anyway.

Nah, too much work. Instead, I spent the next few weeks staring at the calendar, waiting for spring.

Many of the essays in *The New Face of Small-Town America* derive from stories published in the *Allentown Morning Call*. This listing details their original publication information.

1 The Ritual
   "Coming of age: A Latino tradition celebrates a young girl's passage into adulthood." Dec. 1, 2002, A1; national

2 A Principal Duty
   "Lessons learned: After a bumpy start, Roberto Clemente Charter School's principal sees progress. But 'they need so much help, these kids,' he says." Jan. 15, 2001, A1; national

4 Home Away from Home
   "Far afield: Migrants from Mexico who toil in Pennsylvania farms and orchards have picked Shenandoah for their home. The result has been friction in this old Schuylkill County town." Jul. 15, 2001, A1; national

5 Little Hero
   "Little hero: Allentown 7-year-old stands tall as he fights off his sister's attacker." Nov. 19, 2001, A1; local

6 Music to Their Ears
   "Law called culturally biased: Allentown mother of 4 faces eviction under the city's disruptive conduct edict. She says it unfairly targets Latinos." Dec. 3, 2001, B1; local

7 Priceless
   "Tapping the Puerto Rican buying power: Valley merchants find more ways to draw Latino consumers." July 21, 2002, S10; Puerto Rican section

8 The Fearful Side of Business
   "Bethlehem activist seeks to close cultural gaps: She wants people to experience the 'other' South Side, shop there." Feb. 18, 2002, B1; local

9 Side by Side
   "More than one way to be Puerto Rican." July 21, 2002, S14, special Puerto Rico section

10 Blatinos
   "A tale of two identities: The lives of some black Latinos reflect a unique blend of African roots and Hispanic culture. Black History Month." Feb. 26, 2002, B1; local

12 Colorful Pages
"True colors: Responding to a growing ethnic population, libraries acquire more books that reflect a variety of cultures." Feb. 11, 2001, B1; local

13 ABCs
"Learning the lingo: English for Speakers of Other Languages can mean the difference between success and failure for students coming from another culture." May 27, 2001, B1; local

14 Grading the Parents
"Schooling parents: Lehigh Valley districts are trying new ways to get more Latino parents involved in their children's education." Feb. 7, 2002, B1; local

16 Hooked on Telenovelas
"Hooked on tele-novelas: Spanish-speaking viewers prefer TV shows in their native language." Oct. 5, 2001, D1; *AM Magazine*

17 A Step Behind
"Giving children, parents a Head Start: Federally funded program for low-income students helps teach valuable skills to adults, offspring." Dec. 24, 2000, B1; local

18 City Boys
"Life lessons: Dropout learns value of an education. Teen is one of many trying to do better after leaving school." April 21, 2002, B1; local

19 Spanglish
"Conversational mix: New vocabulary evolves from interchangeable use of Spanish and English." March 19, 2002, A1; national

20 The World Trade Connection
"Allentown man relieved his brother survived: Carlos Hamilton, 29, was running downstairs as firemen came upstairs." Sept. 14, 2001, A8; national

21 Latinos Again
"Reviving their roots: A growing number of Latinos in the Lehigh Valley are trying to rediscover their heritage and display it in public." Jan. 15, 2002, B1; local

22 One Man, One Mission
"¡Vaya con Dios! (Go with God!) Brother Alfonso on a mission." Sept. 9, 2001, A1; national

23 Down to Business
"Asian immigrants adapt to an ethnic America: Allentown business owners recognize the importance of being able to speak Spanish." Dec. 29, 2002, B1; local

24 Airwave Wars
"Valley Latino leaders give static to raunchy radio: Spanish-language stations say ratings show listeners want crudeness." July 25, 2002, B1; local

25 Goooaaalll!!!
"Their goal involves more than winning: Lehigh Valley Latin Soccer League players display passion for the game and its traditions." June 18, 2001, B1; local

26 Unfulfilled Dreams
"Unfulfilled dreams: Death of her aunt gives Honduran immigrant a lesson in life." Nov. 10, 2002, B1; local

27 A Rich Life
"Getting ahead in Monroe: County's Latinos live better than many counterparts in other parts of the state." Nov. 29, 2002, B1; local

28 Liberty and Justice for All
"Mixed meanings of the Fourth: Minorities who prosper celebrate their own freedom and opportunity. Others feel that liberty has eluded them." July 2, 2001, A1; national

29 Man of the Cross
"Allentown, Bethlehem churches re-enact the Crucifixion in Good Friday observances: Sacred Heart's Stations of the Cross are narrated in Spanish." Apr. 14, 2001, B3; local

30 Full Circle
"Natives return to their enchanted island: Steel retirees honor their roots in Puerto Rico." July 21, 2002, S6, Puerto Rico section

31 Finding the Inner Snowman
"Glimpses: Finding the inner snowman." Feb. 23, 2001, B1; local

INDEX

Abraczinskas Nurseries, Inc., 18, 19
Adams, Anna, 96
advertising
  Latino market and, 29–31
  shock radio and, 112
  Spanglish used in, 90
African American Latinos, isolation felt by, 41–42
African Americans, alienation of, 128
Agron, Erlinda, 33–35
Allentown
  attractiveness to Latino immigrants, 17–18
  as example of Latino integration, viii
"Allentown" (Joel), vii, ix
Allentown City Council, Latino member of,
  43–45
Allentown public library, books about Latino
  children in, 47, 48
Allentown school district
  number of ESOL students in, 51
  number of Latino students in, 10, 56
Alliance for Building Communities, 27
Almanza, Wilfredo and Marta, 124
Almonte, Rosemary "Boquita," 111
Alu, Mary Ellen, vii
American Legal Defense and Education Fund, 78
Amigas y Rivales (Girlfriend and Rivals), 77, 79
Aparicio, Frances, 95
Arellano, Ramiro, 18
Arey, Kathleen, 29
Argueta, Aneht, 117–21
art, Hispanic, in Lehigh Valley, 15–16
Asian-American businesses, need to cater to
  Latino customers, 105–7
Association of Hispanic Advertising Agencies, 31
Attamian, Cindy, 60

Baird, Scott, 89
Baray, Perla Lopez, 14, 15
barrios. See Latino neighborhoods
Bell, Tyisha, 140
Berger, Esteban, 100–101
Bermudez, Andy, 85–87
Bermudez, Nelson, 3–5
Betancourt, Adelines, 60
Bethlehem, Pennsylvania
  Latino-owned businesses, efforts to boost,
    33–35
  Latino population in, 29

Bethlehem area schools
  outreach to Latino parents, 57
  percentage of Latino students, 56
Bethlehem public library, books about Latino
  children in, 47, 48
Bethlehem Steel, 133–34
black Latinos, isolation felt by, 41–42
Bohorquez, Betty, 60
Bonilla, Alfonso, 99–103
books about bicultural Latino children,
  availability of, 47–49
"born-again Latinos," 95
Boys & Girls Club, 44
Bromley Communications, 90
Burke, Tom, 27–28
businesses
  Latino-owned, efforts to boost, 33–35
  need to cater to Latino customers, 29–31, 105–7
buying power of Latinos, 29–31, 105–7

CADC. *See* Community Action Development
  Committee
Campos, Dr. Luis, 60
Canizares, Rafael, 112
Carita de Angel (Angel Face), 77, 78, 79
Carloni, Lindsey, 35
Castro, Kevin, 42
Catholic brothers, 99–103
Centro de Salud LatinoAmericano (Center for
  Latin American Health), 59–61
Cerullo, Claudio, 9
Chamber of Commerce, Lehigh Valley, 31
change, fear of, viii
Cintron, Iris, 57
City Council, Allentown, Latino member of,
  43–45
Class President (Hurwitz), 49
Clemente, Roberto, 9
cold weather, adapting to, 139–41
Collazo, Rafael, 96, 127–29
college, introducing Latinos to, 44
Colon, Carlos, 90–91
Colon, Ernesto, 134
Colon, Nitza, 55–56
Colon, Pena, 136
Community Action Development Committee
  (CADC), 33, 34, 35
Community Development Department, 25